Motives, Values, Preferences Inventory Manual

2010 Administrative and Norming Updates

Joyce Hogan, Ph.D

Robert Hogan, Ph.D.

Hogan Assessment Systems
Tulsa, OK 74114, USA

2010

Joyce Hogan, Ph.D

Robert Hogan, Ph.D.

Hogan Personality Inventory ™

Hogan Development Survey ™

Motives, Values, Preferences Inventory ™

are the exclusive registered trademarks of

Hogan Assessment Systems, Inc.

www.hoganpress.com

ISBN 978-0-9840969-6-1

HOGANPRESS

TABLE OF CONTENTS

List of Tables and Figures
Tables

Figures

CHAPTER 1

CONCEPTUAL BACKGROUND

Introduction and Definitions

R. S. Peters (1958) points out that we use motivational terms to explain social behavior and argues that motivational terms are explanatory concepts, par excellent. Peters also distinguishes between two categories of motivational terms - causes and reasons - each of which is used to explain social behavior. Causal explanations refer to processes (biological or physiological drives) inside people that somehow propel them into action. Reasons as explanations refer to people's intentions, goals, and preferences; reasons are mental or intrapsychic constructs that explain the direction and focus of people's actions. Although many people regard needs or drives as primary, Peters notes that the concept of need or drive postulates a mysterious end-state of satisfaction or tension reduction that is never measured or observed. He goes on to argue that, for most everyday purposes, we explain a person's behavior in terms of what he or she intends by a course of action. Thus, interests, goals, values, and preferences have a unique role to play in the explanation of social action.

Hogan and Blake (1996) regard needs, values, and interests as closely related concepts. Distinguishing among them seems to be a matter of semantics and personal choice. The terms have been used interchangeably in much of psychology, although values are often seen as the most inclusive construct. Dawis (1980; 1991) notes that authors have equated values with beliefs (Allport, 1961; Rokeach, 1973), attitudes (Campbell, 1966), needs (Maslow, 1954), interests (Allport, 1961; Perry, 1954), and preferences (Katzell, 1964; Rokeach, 1973).

We believe that needs, values, and interests differ primarily in their breadth and level of abstraction. For example, Super (1973) puts needs at the most abstract level of the hierarchy. He sees values and interests as lower-order constructs that are derived from needs. He defines values as objectives sought to satisfy needs and he defines interests as the specific activities and objects through which individuals pursue values and satisfies their needs. Interests, then, are the least abstract constructs in Super's hierarchy of motivational terms.

Dawis (1980) suggests that interests, attitudes, needs, values, and preferences belong to a set of constructs that represent "an affective orientation toward stimulus objects" (p. 77). Like Super, he suggests the constructs are arranged in a hierarchy: "Attitudes appear to be the most general construct and refer to a favorable-unfavorable (accept-reject) orientation toward attitude objects. Needs and values refer to the importance-unimportance of the stimulus object. By contrast, preferences and interests refer to the dimension of liking-disliking for the stimulus object" (p. 77). Although there are some differences between Dawis' and Super's hierarchies, they both regard interests as the most specific construct in a hierarchy of motivational terms.

The higher-order constructs must be translated into specific exemplars to be assessed. Thus, to measure the need for achievement, one must identify the values, preferences, and interests that characterize that need - e.g., valuing success and accomplishment, preferring recognition over anonymity, and being interested in competitive activities. Assessing constructs at the lowest level of the hierarchy does not require inferences about their relationships to higher-order constructs. For example, interpreting the item "I like tennis" requires no assumptions about the motives or goals that explain a person's attraction to the sport; that preference could be based on any of a number of underlying motives. Klinger's (1977) distinction between "needs" and "current concerns" seems relevant. According to Klinger:

> . . . a need or motive such as "achievement" or "affiliation" can subsume a wide range of possible concrete goals, any one of which may be the focus of a current concern. Thus, someone with a high "need to achieve" may have separate current concerns about setting a new sales record, beating his or her tennis partner, and patenting a new design for a mousetrap. On the other hand, someone interested in setting a new sales record may be doing it for the money, not because of a need to achieve. (p. 350)

Thus, connecting interests with more abstract motivational constructs may be difficult; being interested in an activity can stem from any number of more abstract motives. More importantly, interests can predict behavior without identifying a higher-order construct to explain the prediction. That is, in fact, how vocational interest measurement developed. Moreover, a considerable empirical literature demonstrates the predictive utility of vocational interest measures. Thus far, however, there seems to have been comparatively little progress in connecting interests to constructs in other domains (Dawis, 1980; 1991; Holland, 1976). Holland notes the separation of interest measurement from the rest of psychology with marked dissatisfaction:

> The interest literature still remains largely outside the mainstream of psychology and sociology. The sheer empirical success of these inventories may have relieved interest enthusiasts of the need to cultivate other parts of psychology. Subsequently, neither group - interest types and the other types in psychology - have developed useful dependencies upon one another. Consequently, the interest literature remains a rambling, formless literature integrated only by a few popular inventories and unable to draw on the strengths of personality and learning theory and vice versa. (p. 523)

The foregoing discussion can be summarized in three points. First, the definitions of needs, values, and interests overlap substantially. Second, these terms can be placed in a hierarchy of abstraction with interests as the most concrete and values as the most abstract. And third, although philosophers regard these terms as crucial for explaining social action, psychologists have been largely uninterested in their philosophical implications - specifically, psychologists seem not to understand that: (a) it is tautological to explain behavior in terms of traits, but (b) it is meaningful to explain behavior in terms of values, preferences, and interests (Peters, 1958).

The Meaning of Interests

The history of interest measurement primarily concerns efforts to demonstrate its utility. This effort may have been driven by the fact that interest measurement was initially seen as a questionable enterprise. E. K. Strong (1943) observed that ". . . some people in various walks of life, including psychologists, have considered the study of interests as 'of no scientific value,' 'extremely silly and pernicious stuff,' 'a sheer waste of time,' 'useless and inane'" (p. 8). Perhaps in response to such criticisms, interest measurement research emphasized the ability of such measures to predict meaningful outcomes - work satisfaction, occupational tenure, vocational choice, and so on. Researchers also investigated the stability of vocational interests as well as the covariance structures underlying the items and scales of various interest inventories. As a result, theory - about what interests are - took a back seat to empiricism. Strong defined interests solely in terms of responses to interest test items. According to Strong (1960), interests are:

> . . . activities that are liked or disliked. Each person engages in thousands of activities, or habits, if you prefer that term, and attached to each is a liking-disliking affective tone. They remind me of tropisms. We go toward liked activities, go away from disliked activities. (p. 12)

Although many people regard the interest literature as conceptually barren, Strong's statement contains an implicit assumption about the motivational nature of interests; he regards them as having "directional" properties. In another statement, Strong (1955) acknowledged both the practical concerns that drove the construction of interest inventories (i.e., career guidance and placement) and the conceptual/theoretical connection between interests and other theories of human motivation:

> Interest scores measure a complex of liked and disliked activities selected so as to differentiate members of an occupation from non-members. Such a complex is equivalent to a "condition which supplies stimulation for a particular type of behavior, "i.e., toward or away from participation in the activities characteristic of a given occupation. Interest scores are consequently measures of drives. (p. 142)

Personality and Interests

We noted above that interests represent the lower level of a hierarchy of motivational constructs - a personality hierarchy of increasing abstractness and decreasing specificity as one moves to successively higher levels. The notion that personality and interests are related or even equivalent has always appealed to vocational psychologists. Hansen (1984) characterizes the notion as "one of the most enduring hypotheses within interest measurement" (p. 116), and virtually all the major players in this field have, at one time or another, suggested that interests reflect more basic person-ality characteristics. Darley and Hagenah (1955), for example, regarded vocational interest measurement as "a special case in personality theory" and proposed that "interests reflect, in the vocabulary of the world of work, the value systems, the needs, and the motivations of individuals" (p. 191). Layton (1958) considered interests to be "one aspect of what is broadly considered as the motivation of an individual . . . a part of the person's personality structure or organization" (p. 3-4). Bordin (1943) regarded interest inventory scores as measures of "self concept." Strong (1955) described interest scores as measures of "drives" (p. 142). Super and Crites (1962) suggested that interests have a biological basis - interests are "the product of interaction between inherited neural and endocrine factors, on the one hand, and opportunity and social evaluation on the other" (p. 410). Roe (1957; Roe & Siegelman, 1964) suggested that parental relations during early childhood produces an orientation toward either "persons" or "nonpersons" that, in turn, affects the development of an individual's pattern of interests.

Holland (1973) made the strongest statement regarding the relationships between interests and personality:

> If vocational interests are construed as an expression of personality, then they represent the expression of personality in work, school subjects, hobbies, recreational activities, and preferences. In short, what we have called "vocational interests" are simply another aspect of personality . . . If vocational interests are an expression of personality, then it follows that interest inventories are personality inventories. (p. 7)

Nonetheless, the content of the two types of inventories - interests versus personality - suggest that they sample something different. Hofstee (1990) notes that the prototypical personality questionnaire item is a "conditional" trait, "an expressed predisposition to behave in a certain way in a particular situation" (p. 79). He also notes that personality inventory items typically consist of "a hodgepodge of descriptions of overt and covert reactions, trait attributions, wishes and interests, biographical facts, attitudes and beliefs, descriptions of others' reactions to the subject, and more or less bizarre opinions (e.g., 'Somebody is trying to poison me')" (p. 79). In contrast, Rounds (1995) describes the content of interest items and scales as follows:

> Broadly speaking, interest items and scales involve preferences for behaviors (response and activity families), situations (the context in which the preferred behaviors occur, usually occupations or physical settings), and reinforcer systems (outcomes or reinforcers associated with the behavior in the situation). On the response side, vocational interests are usually characterized by a shared property of the activities (Selling, Technical Writing, Teaching), and are often implied in the objects of interest (Mathematics, Physical Science, Religion) or inferred as a latent entity (Enterprising, Inquiring, Leading- Influencing); on the stimulus side a shared property of the context (Outdoor Work, Office Work, Industrial) is invoked to explain interest covariation. . . . (p. 184-188)

The conventional wisdom is that personality inventories measure traits whereas interest inventories measure preferences. Our view is closer to Bordin's (1943) - we think both kinds of inventories measure self-concepts. Hogan (1983, 1995) points out that when people respond to items on psychological inventories, they behave much as they do during other forms of social interaction.

People use their responses to tell others about their idealized self-concept - about how they would like to be regarded by other people. Here, however, we come to a crucial difference between personality and interest inventories. Personality measures ask about a person's typical response in various situations, but interest measures ask about a person's preferred activities, roles, and associates. Interest measures allow people to describe themselves as they would like to be. Thus, interest inventories get much closer to the content of a person's self-concept than do personality measures.

Interest inventories also allow people to describe themselves in a manner more consistent with their behavior when interacting with strangers. Consider a conversation between people who have just met in an informal social situation. In response to the inquiry "Tell me about yourself," a person is more likely to say "I like tennis" than "In most situations, I am highly competitive." People are accustomed to talking about themselves in terms of interests; interests are at the core of the language of social self-description.

Structure of Interests

According to Rounds (1995), factor analyses of the interest domain suggests it has a roughly hierarchical structure with approximately three levels of generality. At the lowest level are occupational interest factors; each factor is a set of activities that characterize a particular work setting or occupation; "Elementary Education" and "Library Science" are examples of occupational interest factors. At a more general level are what Rounds calls basic interest dimensions. According to Rounds, these "comprise work activities that transcend particular situations (occupations)" (p. 188). These dimensions seem to emerge most reliably from item-level factor analyses of vocational interest inventories, and include factors like "mechanical activities," "mathematics," or "outdoor activities." The activities that form these factors seem intuitively similar, and Rounds notes that "most people describe their vocational interests using the language of basic interests" (p. 188).

Finally, at the highest level are "general interest factors." These typically emerge from higher-order analyses of basic interest dimensions. At this level, "the elements of the activity family (or occupational family) are dissimilar and an internal entity is postulated to explain their covariation" (Rounds, 1995, p. 188).

Rounds (1995) suggests that, for the interest domain, the distinction between basic interest dimensions and the general interest themes corresponds to Meehl's (1986) distinction between "surface" and "source" traits. Scales designed to measure the higher-order, general interest themes have only recently become part of interest inventories. This process is reflected in the successive revisions of the Strong Interest Inventory (SII). It began as a series of empirically-keyed occupational scales, but the current form of the SII contains scales corresponding to all three of the levels proposed by Rounds.

Although Strong (1943), Roe (1956), Holland (1973), and Jackson (1977) have proposed general interest schemes, Holland's system is the most widely accepted and popular in the U.S. Building on Roe's work and factor-analyses reported by Guilford, Christensen, Bond, and Sutton (1954), Holland (1973, 1985a) proposed a taxonomy for organizing individuals and occupations using six occupational "personality types." Realistic (R) types are practical, hands on, real world and action oriented; Investigative (I) types are abstract, analytical, and theory oriented; Artistic (A) types are imaginative, impractical, and try to entertain, amuse, and fascinate others; Social (S) types enjoy helping, serving, and assisting others; Enterprising (E) types try to manipulate, persuade, and outperform others; and Conventional (C) types count, regulate, and organize people or things. The types are portrayed in a hexagonal configuration; adjacent types are more similar to one another than are types located at opposite sides of the hexagon. Although multidimensional analyses of scales designed to measure Holland's types rarely, if ever, reproduce a perfectly shaped hexagon, they generally replicate a circumplicial ordering of the types (i.e., RIASEC), suggesting that the internal relations among the types match Holland's model (Dawis, 1991; Rounds, Davison, & Dawis, 1979; Rounds & Zevon, 1983). Alternative structural models summarizing the relations among the types have been proposed (e.g., Gati, 1991), but the evidence consistently supports Holland's hexagonal model as the most adequate representation of the structure of interests (Tracey & Rounds, 1992).

In the domain of interest measurement, Holland's model has attained about the same status as the Five-Factor Model or Big-Five in personality assessment. Holland's model has also had a major impact on the construction of interest inventories; in addition to Holland's own tests - the Vocational Preference Inventory (VPI; Holland, 1965) and Self-Directed Search (SDS; Holland, 1985b) - most other inventories report their results in Holland's terms. In the early 1970's, Holland's scales were incorporated into the Strong-Campbell Interest Inventory (now Strong Interest Inventory; SII; Campbell & Holland, 1972; Hansen & Johannson, 1972). Subsequently, authors of other inventories, notably the Unisex Edition of the ACT Interest Inventory (UNIACT; ACT Inc., 1981), the Career Assessment Inventory, Vocational Edition (CAI-V; Johannson, 1986), and the Career Decision-Making Inventory (CDM; Harrington & O'Shea, 1982) have developed measures of Holland's themes. Even Kuder, who has his own organizational scheme, provides formulas to translate his scores into Holland's themes (Zytowski & Kuder, 1986). Although Roe developed a model that is in many ways similar to Holland's scheme, it has not achieved the same degree of popularity.

Interests and Occupational Criteria

Strong (1943) noted that he could think of "no better criterion for a vocational interest test than that of satisfaction enduring over a period of time" (p. 385). Occupational membership - which implies satisfaction - has been the most popular dependent variable in the study of interests. Research consistently finds that members of different occupations respond differently to interest items, and many occupational groups can be distinguished on the basis of their interests. Furthermore, occupational membership can be reliably predicted from interests measured at an earlier age. Strong (1935, 1943) reports long term follow-up studies with the Strong Vocational Interest Bank (SVIB) yielding impressive "hit rates" (as high as 78%) in predicting occupational membership using interest scale scores obtained five to eighteen years earlier. Strong's findings have been replicated by many investigators using a variety of samples and methods (e.g., Bartling & Hood, 1981; Brandt & Hood, 1968; Cairo, 1982; Campbell, 1966; Dolliver, Irvin, & Bigley, 1972; Dolliver & Will, 1977; Gade & Soliah, 1975; Hansen, 1986; Hansen & Swanson, 1983; Lau & Abrahams, 1971; Worthington & Dolliver, 1977; Zytowski, 1976). There is solid evidence that measured interests predict occupational membership criteria.

Although these results are impressive, they nonetheless raise questions about the factors that explain a person's tenure in a particular occupation. Dawis and Lofquist (1984) propose that two relatively distinct appraisal processes affect tenure in an occupation. One is the degree to which a person is satisfied with the environment - the nature of the work, the working conditions, the compensation, the quality of relationships with coworkers and supervisors. The other is the degree to which the environment (i.e., the employer) is satisfied with the employee. The implications of these appraisals for tenure are relatively straightforward. A dissatisfied employee will be more likely to leave an occupation or organization; an unsatisfactory employee will be more likely to be expelled. A more fine-grained analysis of the relationship between interests and occupational success requires that the validity of measured interests for each of these criteria be considered separately.

Satisfaction

As noted above, Strong (1943) believed that the most appropriate criterion for assessing the validity of interest measures is satisfaction. Research on this topic, however, has produced mixed results. A number of researchers have failed to find a significant relationship between interests and job satisfaction (e.g., Bartling & Hood, 1981; Butler, Crinnion, & Martin, 1972; Cairo, 1982; Dolliver et al., 1972; McArthur, 1954; Schletzer, 1966; Trimble, 1965; Zytowski, 1976). Others, however, have found the expected relationships (e.g., Barak & Meir, 1974; DeMichael & Dabelstein, 1947; Hahn & Williams, 1945; Herzberg & Russell, 1953; Klein & Weiner, 1977; McRae, 1959; North, 1958; Trimble, 1965; Worthington & Dolliver, 1977). In the positive studies, the correlations have generally been low to moderate. Barge and Hough (1988) cite 18 studies with a median correlation of .31 between interests and job satisfaction.

Campbell (1971) suggests that the modest relationships between interests and job satisfaction reported in the literature reflect a restriction in the range of the criterion variable; i.e., most incumbents express satisfaction with their work. Weaver (1980), for example, reports that more than 80% of American workers said they were either somewhat or very satisfied with their jobs. It is also becoming clear that a variety of factors influence workers' judgments about whether a job is "satisfying." It is not clear that having "interesting work" is a major concern for all employees. Moreover, many features of the work environment - i.e., pay, security, supervision - that have little to do with the content of the work also influence satisfaction. Furthermore, there are marked individual differences in the degree to which any of these factors influence workers' feelings of satisfaction with a job (Dawis & Lofquist, 1984). Finally, there are individual differences in the degree to which workers express satisfaction with any job; individual differences in the disposition to experience positive or negative affective states strongly influence self-reported job satisfaction (e.g., Burke, Brief, & George, 1993; Costa & McCrae, 1980; Levin & Stokes, 1989).

Satisfactoriness

There is little systematic research on the link between interests and the degree to which an employee is regarded by others as satisfactory. Nonetheless, existing studies yield reasonable validity coefficients. Most studies use performance ratings as criteria and involve a variety of occupational groups including: Navy enlisted personnel (Borman, Toquam, & Rosse, 1979; Dann & Abrahams, 1977; Lau & Abrahams, 1970); Naval Academy cadets (Abrahams & Neumann, 1973); forest rangers (Miner, 1960); supervisors (Strong, 1943); foremen and assistant foremen (Schultz & Barnabas, 1945); managers (Johnson & Dunnette, 1968; Nash, 1966); engineers (Dunnette & Aylward, 1956); counselors (Wiggins & Weslander, 1979). Barge and Hough (1988) review the results of 11 studies using performance ratings as the dependent variable and report correlations ranging from .01 to .40 (median r = .20). There is variability even within a single study; Lau and Abrahams (1970), in a study of Navy enlisted recruits report, for example, correlations between interest scores and performance ratings ranging from .15 to .38 (median r = .25). Although there are occasional negative findings (e.g., Dunnette & Aylward, 1956), the validity coefficients compare favorably with those obtained with personality inventories and are occasionally quite large. Wiggins and Weslander (1979) report correlations of -.60 and .56 between the Realistic and Social scales of Holland's VPI and the rated performance of counselors.

Productivity

A handful of studies have found positive relations between interests and objective indices of worker productivity. Three of the studies cited by Barge and Hough (1988) used archival production records as dependent variables, and found a median correlation between interests and performance of .33 (range from .24 to .53). Strong (1943) reported a correlation of .40 between interest scores and the productivity of insurance agents. Knauft (1951) reported a cross-validated correlation of .53 between a specially developed key and an objective criterion of performance (cost/sales ratio) for bakery shop managers. Clark (1961) concluded that work performance is an interaction between ability and interests; Clark's data indicated that interest scores predict job performance better at some ability levels than at others.

Organizational Climate

Holland (1973, 1985a) and Schneider (1987) suggest that, in order to understand organizational behavior, we need to understand the values, interests, and personalities of an organization's members. Holland argues that "the character of an environment reflects the typical characteristics of its members. If we know what kind of people make up a group, we can infer the climate the group creates" (1985a, p. 35). Similarly, Schneider argues that organizations attract, select, and retain particular kinds of people, and that the climate of an organization is a function of the kind of people it retains. Pfeffer's (1983) "organizational demography model" is similar, but focuses on the shared biographical characteristics of incumbents. In each of these schemes, interpersonal compatibility determines an individual's "fit" with an organization. Consistent with the social psychological literature, interpersonal compatibility is associated with perceived similarity, and this, in turn, produces a relative homogeneity of values and interests within organizations. Both Holland and Schneider define the climate of an organization in terms of the members' characteristics rather than their requisite tasks. They also suggest that taxonomies of work environments based on worker characteristics may predict work outcomes better than taxonomies based on task characteristics; person analysis may be more important than task analysis.

There is substantial empirical support for these ideas in the vocational interest literature. The notion that interpersonal similarity is psychologically important and that, "birds of a feather flock together" is a cornerstone of vocational psychology (Darley & Hagenah, 1955, p. 19). Holland's (1973) taxonomy defines occupational environments in terms of members' interests and values. The model also predicts how compatible individuals will be with others in a particular occupational or organizational setting - and this in turn predicts how others in the work environment will react to that individual. To the extent that individual success depends on others' reactions to - and subjective evaluations of - an incumbent, interest inventories are likely to be effective as job placement tools.

In summary, it is useful to know what kinds of people make up an occupation (or organization). It is also useful to be able to predict how compatible an individual will be with others in an occupation (or organization). The field of vocational interest measurement reflects a perspective on the individual that is quite different from that in industrial-organizational psychology. Vocational psychologists help people find compatible work environments. That involves helping a person choose from among an array of employment options - and matching individual differences to characteristics of occupations. Vocational counseling required the development of a taxonomy of work environments. Holland's taxonomy is one example of a psychologically meaningful taxonomy of work environments (cf., Borgen, Weiss, Tinsley, Dawis, & Lofquist, 1968; Dawis, Dohm, Lofquist, Chartrand, & Due, 1987; Rosen, Weiss, Hendel, Dawis, & Lofquist, 1972). Industrial/organizational psychology has yet to avail itself of much of this work. Nevertheless, the advantages of these taxonomic schemes for researchers undertaking meta-analyses in order to uncover important relationships between individual differences and important work outcomes should be obvious.

Summary

This chapter makes three major points. First, motivational constructs can be organized in a roughly hierarchical structure; abstract intentional concepts (values) occupy the highest level of the hierarchy and the concrete manifestation of those intentions (interests) occupies the lowest level. Second, the pattern of an individual's preferences, as seen in his or her responses to an inventory of values and interests, has important real world consequences; interests are demonstrably associated with vocational success and satisfaction. Although we have discussed these notions only in general terms, more specific information about motivational constructs is presented in the next chapters. And third, values and interests are motivational concepts. If we know what a person values and what he or she finds interesting, then we know a great deal about him or her - we have a powerful tool for understanding, advising, and/or managing that person.

CHAPTER 2

INVENTORY CONSTRUCTION

What to Measure

The Motives, Values, Preferences Inventory (MVPI) is designed to serve two very important goals. First, the MVPI permits an evaluation of the fit between an individual and the organizational culture. This is quite important because, no matter how talented and hard working a person may be, if his or her values are incompatible with the values of the larger culture - and the culture is usually defined by the values of top management - then he or she will not do well in the organization.

Second, the MVPI is unique among the inventories that are currently available in that it directly assesses a person's motives (Hogan, J., & Hogan, 1996). The standard interest measures allow inference about a person's motives on the basis of his or her expressed occupational choices. But from the MVPI, one can determine immediately the degree to which, for example, a person is motivated by money, security, or fun. The only alternative to the MVPI for directly assessing a person's motives is to use a projective measure.

The scales of the MVPI represent dimensions that have historic presence in the literature on motivation. We reviewed 80 years of theory and research on motives, values, and interests and developed 10 content scales. We were specifically influenced by the taxonomies of Spranger (1928), Allport (1961), Murray (1938), Allport, Vernon, and Lindzey (1960), and Holland (1966, 1985a). Although the authors use different labels to orient their taxonomies and some of their dimensions are trait-like while others refer to types, there is, nonetheless, considerable overlap in the attitudes, values, needs, interests, goals, and commitments that they regard as important. Gregory (1992) summarizes these motivational constructs (see Table 2.1) and indicates how their content aligns with the 10 scales of the MVPI.

Because the history of each of these constructs is useful for understanding measurement goals for each MVPI scale, we highlight some of the views that have influenced what we believe to be an adequate taxonomy of motives.

Table 2.1

Logical Taxonomy of Motives, Attitudes, Values, Needs, Interests, Goals, and Commitments

	Attitudes: Spranger	Values: Allport, Vernon, & Lindzey	Needs: Murray	Interests: Holland	Goals: Richards	Goals: Wicker, Lambert, Richardson, & Kahler	Goals: Pervin	Commitments: Novacek & Lazarus
Aesthetic	Aesthetic	Aesthetic	Sentience	Artistic	Artistic			Sensation-Seeking
Affiliation	Social	Social	Affiliation	Social			Relaxation-Fun-Friendship	Affiliation
Altruistic	Social	Social	Nurturance	Social	Altruistic	Interpersonal Concern	Affection-Support	Altruism
Commercial	Economic	Economic	Acquisition	Conventional				Power/Achievement
Hedonistic	Aesthetic		Sex, Play		Hedonistic		Relaxation-Fun-Friendship	Sensation-Seeking
Power	Political	Political	Achievement Dominance	Enterprising	Prestige	Competitive Ambition	Aggression-Power	Power/Achievement
Recognition	Political	Political	Exhibition		Prestige	Competitive Ambition	Aggression-Power	Power/Achievement
Scientific	Theoretical	Theoretical	Understanding	Investigative	Scientific			
Security			Succorance Infavoidance	Conventional			Reduce Tension-Conflict-Threat	Stress Avoidance
Tradition	Religious	Religious			Religious			Personal Growth

Note. Source: Gregory (1992). Reprinted with permission.

Aesthetic Motives

Spranger's (1928) conception of the aesthete was a person who enjoys the pleasures of the body and the arts. Murray's (1938) need for sentience, which he described as seeking out sensuous feelings and impressions, is similar to Spranger's aesthetic attitude. Holland's (1987, p. 5) artistic type values the world of beauty, identifies with artists of various disciplines, and aspires to work in artistic pursuits. Holland describes artistic types as creative, sensitive, imaginative, and nonconforming.

Affiliation Motives

Spranger's (1928) social attitude highlights desires for interaction and positive interpersonal relations. Murray's (1938) need for affiliation is one of the best known motives in his taxonomy; it emphasizes a desire for friendship. Holland's (1987) social type wants to be helpful, identifies with do-gooders/bleeding hearts, and seeks out opportunities for social interaction.

Altruistic Motives

Altruistic motives resemble affiliation motives; Spranger's (1928) social attitude and Holland's (1987) social type capture part of this construct. However, the distinction between affiliation and altruism is nicely characterized in Murray's (1938) need for nurturance. Nurturance focuses on helping, protecting, caring for, and curing those in need while affiliation concerns desires for friendship and being around others. Novacek and Lazarus (1990) identified a dimension called altruism which they describe as the desire to help and support others as well as being willing to make sacrifices for them.

Commercial Motives

Interest in business and money making are the keys to commercial motives and this dimension can be traced back to Spranger's (1928) economic attitude, which emphasized the desire to control resources and to acquire material possessions. Allport et al. (1960) economic man is interested in business and the accumulation of wealth. Holland's (1987) conventional type is interested in business, identifies with successful business people, and wants to work in finance and commerce. These types are described as conservative, conforming, unimaginative, and methodical.

Hedonistic Motives

None of Spranger's (1928) attitudes are closely aligned with hedonistic motives. Murray's (1938) needs for sex and play contain elements that are similar to hedonism; erotic pleasure is the basis of the need for sex and having fun is the basis of the need for play. Holland (1987) has no type analogous to the hedonistic motive. Novacek and Lazarus (1990) identify a sensation seeking dimension that emphasizes sexual pleasure, fun, free time, and excitement.

Power Motives

Spranger's (1928) political attitude highlights achievement, aggression, status, and dominance. Allport et al. (1960) describes the political man as one who primarily focuses on achieving power. Murray's (1938) needs for achievement and dominance fit closely with the power motive. The power motive is clearly aligned with Holland's (1987) enterprising type. This type seeks leadership positions, values freedom and ambition, and has as a life goal of being in charge. Holland describes enterprising types as power-seeking, dominant, enthusiastic, and energetic.

Recognition Motives

The need to be recognized and to gain the attention of others is distinct from the power motive. Although Spranger (1928), Allport et al. (1960), and Novacek and Lazarus (1990) combine power with recognition, Murray (1938) distinguishes between power and recognition by proposing achievement and dominance needs (power) and exhibition needs (recognition). Gregory (1992) proposes that recognition may apply to all of Holland's (1987) types, since the theme tends to resemble a trait more than a type.

Scientific Motives

Spranger's (1928) theoretical attitude emphasizes a preference for naming, classifying, and logical analysis. Similarly, Allport et al. (1960) proposed that the theoretical man seeks to discover truth through empirical, critical, and logical means. Holland's (1987) investigative type values logic, analysis, and the pursuit of knowledge. This type enjoys science and identifies with scientists. Holland describes the investigative type as intellectual, scholarly, analytical, and curious.

Security Motives

As seen in Table 2.1, the security motives are not well-mapped by constructs identified by the major motivational theorists. Gregory (1992) points out that these motives are also more like traits than types. Because the construct concerns needs for certainty, control and order, it resembles Murray's (1938) definition of the needs for succorance and infavoidance. The succorance need entails the desire to be protected and cared for, whereas the infavoidance need implies a cautious, controlled attitude. There is some overlap between the security motives and Holland's description of conventional types as conforming, conservative, and methodical.

Tradition Motives

The tradition motives resemble Spranger's (1928) religious attitudes which are concerned with moral issues and conservative values. Novacek and Lazarus (1990) identified a personal growth dimension that contains the moral, ethical, and spiritual themes associated with the tradition motives, particularly in the aspiration to be fair and just, and the need to develop a philosophy of life. None of Holland's (1987) types endorse the tradition motives, with the possible exception of social types, who are idealistic, want to help others, value equality, and identify with spiritual leaders.

Definitions of the Scales

The 10 MVPI scales are defined as follows:

Aesthetic motives are associated with an interest in art, literature, music, the humanities and a lifestyle guided by questions of culture, good taste, and attractive surroundings.

Affiliation motives are associated with a desire for and enjoyment of social interaction.

Altruistic motives involve concern about the welfare of others, especially the less fortunate, a desire to help them, and in some way, contribute to the development of a better society.

Commercial motives reflect an interest in business and business-related matters such as accounting, marketing, management, and finances.

Hedonistic motives produce an orientation toward fun, pleasure, and enjoyment.

Power motives are associated with a desire for success, accomplishment, status, competition, and control.

Recognition motives reflect responsiveness to attention, approval, praise, and a need to be recognized.

Scientific motives are associated with a desire for knowledge, an enthusiasm for new and advanced technologies, and a curiosity about how things work.

Security motives reflect a desire for certainty, predictability, order, and control in one's life.

Tradition motives are typically expressed in terms of a dedication to ritual, history, and old-fashioned virtues.

Composition of the MVPI

The MVPI contains 200 items in the form of statements to which a respondent indicates "agree," "uncertain," or "disagree." Each scale contains 20 items that were derived rationally from hypotheses about the likes, dislikes, and aversions of the "ideal" exemplar of each motive. Each scale is composed of five themes: (a) Lifestyles, which concern the manner in which a person would like to live; (b) Beliefs, which involve "shoulds," ideals, and ultimate life goals; (c) Occupational Preferences, which include the work an individual would like to do, what constitutes a good job, and preferred work materials; (d) Aversions, which reflect attitudes and behaviors that are either disliked or distressing; and (e) Preferred Associates, which include the kind of persons desired as coworkers and friends.

There are no correct or incorrect responses for the MVPI scales; therefore, there is no need for validity or faking keys. There is no item overlap among the 10 scales. The items were screened for invasive and offensive content. There are no items concerning sexual preferences, criminal or illegal behavior, racial/ethnic attitudes, or attitudes about disabled individuals. There are no items that could be used to determine physical or mental disabilities; the MVPI is not a medical examination. Readability statistics conducted on the 200 items indicated an average sentence length of 9.7 words and an average word length of 4.7 characters. The Flesch-Kincaid reading level analysis shows that the inventory is written at the third grade level. The MVPI items are easy to understand and are face valid (Feltham & Loan-Clarke, 2007).

MVPI Scale Descriptives

Table 2.2 presents descriptive statistics and reliabilities for each of the MVPI scales. Because the response coding uses a 3-point scale (1 = disagree, 2 = uncertain, 3 = agree), and each scale contains 20 items, scale scores range from 20 to 60. With the exception of the test-retest reliabilities, the data in Table 2.2 are based on an archival sample of 3,015 adults, most of whom are job applicants or employees. Table 2.2 indicates that the highest mean scale scores occur on the Altruistic, Affiliation, and Power scales, respectively. The lowest mean scores occur on the Aesthetic, Hedonistic, and Scientific scales. The Aesthetic scale is the most variable (SD = 8.02), whereas the Affiliation scale is the least variable (SD = 5.56). Internal consistency or alpha reliabilities (Cronbach, 1951) vary between .70 (Security) and .84 (Aesthetic) with an average alpha of .77. Overall, the MVPI has good internal consistency reliability (Feltham & Loan-Clarke, 2007; Roberts, 2001).

Table 2.2

Descriptive Statistics and Reliabilities for the MVPI

	Number of items	Mean	SD	Alpha	Inter-Item r
Aesthetic	20	34.5	8.02	.84	.22
Affiliation	20	49.1	5.56	.71	.14
Altruistic	20	50.7	6.53	.81	.19
Commercial	20	44.6	6.41	.71	.11
Hedonistic	20	38.0	6.83	.78	.14
Power	20	47.6	6.00	.71	.11
Recognition	20	43.2	7.11	.77	.14
Scientific	20	40.2	7.61	.80	.16
Security	20	43.1	6.46	.70	.11
Tradition	20	46.5	7.12	.80	.16

Test-Retest Reliability

The data for our test-retest reliability analyses were drawn exclusively from working adults who completed the MVPI on multiple occasions. Although we have test-retest data over periods extending from 1 day to 5 years, it is proposed that the two durations that are most practically useful for employers and users of the MVPI are (a) less than 3 months between test sessions and (b) between 9 to 12 months between test sessions. Most retesting within an organization takes place in a timeframe of one year or less.

Short-Term Stability (less than 3 months)

This test-retest group consists of 234 cases, including 127 males, 77 females, and 30 individuals who did not provide gender information. Nine percent designated themselves as Black, 2.5% as Hispanic, 6% as Asian, 1% as "Two or More Races", and 53.5% as White. The mean age of this group was 34.47 years with a standard deviation of 10.35 years. As shown in Table 2.3, short-term reliability of MVPI scales range from .71 (Power) to .85 (Aesthetic). Gregory (1992) obtained similar results, evaluating test-retest scale stability over an eight week interval.

Long-Term Stability (between 9 to 12 months)

This test-retest group consists of 129 cases, including 81 males, 39 females, and 9 individuals who did not provide gender information. Eight percent designated themselves as Black, 5% as Hispanic, 4.5% as Asian, 1% as "Two or More Races," and 62% as White. The mean age of this group was 33.01 years with a standard deviation of 9.84 years. As shown in Table 2.3, long-term reliability of MVPI scales range from .70 (Hedonistic, Tradition) to .83 (Security).

Table 2.3 presents Pearson correlation coefficients which summarize the stability of the MVPI scale scores over time. Looking at these results, it is clear that there is a high degree of similarity between test scores across two occasions for both short- and long-term intervals.

Table 2.3

Short- and Long-Term Stability Coefficients for the MVPI

MVPI Scale	Pearson Correlations	
	< = 3 months	9-12 months
Aesthetic	.85	.82
Affiliation	.76	.73
Altruistic	.80	.71
Commercial	.81	.79
Hedonistic	.77	.70
Power	.71	.78
Recognition	.74	.82
Scientific	.82	.76
Security	.80	.83
Tradition	.81	.70

Note. Short-Term N = 234; Long-Term N = 129.

Demographic Differences

Table 2.4 contains scale means and standard deviations by gender, race/ethnicity, and age. As seen, men and women obtain comparable scores across all scales; the largest mean difference is slightly more than 2 points on the Scientific scale in favor of men, and less than 3 points on the Aesthetic scale in favor of women. The largest race differences occur on the Security and Recognition scales with Blacks scoring slightly higher than Whites. Comparing younger and older individuals, those under 40 years have slightly higher mean scores for Hedonistic and Recognition motives, while those 40 years and older have higher average scores for Security and Tradition motives. Because the sample sizes are so large, significance tests of group differences are meaningless and, therefore, are not presented.

Table 2.4

Raw Score Means and Standard Deviations for MVPI Scales by Demographic Group

	Male		Female		Black		White		Under 40		40 & Above	
	Mean	SD	Mean	SD	Mean	SD	Mean	SD	Mean	SD	Mean	SD
Aesthetic	33.7	7.85	36.5	8.10	34.4	7.82	33.8	7.88	34.5	8.20	33.8	7.38
Affiliation	49.2	5.47	48.7	5.80	48.0	5.12	49.9	5.12	49.1	5.59	49.4	5.32
Altruistic	50.8	6.57	50.6	6.41	52.2	6.10	50.6	6.28	51.2	6.38	49.5	6.31
Commercial	45.1	6.41	43.1	6.13	46.2	6.64	44.5	6.40	44.4	6.52	45.4	5.88
Hedonistic	37.8	6.92	38.7	6.59	37.5	6.09	37.1	6.39	38.7	6.91	35.3	5.88
Power	48.1	5.72	46.2	6.44	47.6	5.50	47.6	6.02	47.8	5.85	47.7	6.38
Recognition	43.6	7.05	41.9	7.12	44.5	6.85	42.5	7.02	43.8	6.96	41.5	7.33
Scientific	40.8	7.44	38.4	7.71	38.9	6.80	39.8	7.59	40.6	7.63	39.8	7.34
Security	43.3	6.41	42.6	6.55	46.1	5.89	42.4	6.52	43.5	6.29	52.0	6.65
Tradition	46.5	7.28	46.3	6.72	48.3	6.66	47.1	6.90	46.2	7.16	48.1	6.93

Table 2.5 presents the correlations between the MVPI scales based on a sample of 3,015 respondents. As seen, Commercial is positively correlated with every other MVPI scale, which may reflect a status dimension running through the scales. Similarly, Power and Recognition correlate to some degree with every scale except Security and Tradition. All scales have about three meaningful correlations with other scales. The only inverse relation in the matrix is the correlation of -.30 between Hedonistic and Tradition, which is appropriate and meaningful.

Table 2.5

MVPI Scale Intercorrelations

	AES	AFF	ALT	CML	HDN	PWR	REC	SCI	SEC	TRA
Aesthetic	—									
Affiliation	-.03	—								
Altruistic	.12	.39	—							
Commercial	.10	.19	.10	—						
Hedonistic	.25	.09	-.03	.14	—					
Power	.12	.32	.20	.48	.25	—				
Recognition	.22	.27	.13	.33	.43	.50	—			
Scientific	.33	-.02	.11	.25	.11	.28	.21	—		
Security	-.10	-.02	.30	.25	-.04	.06	.02	.06	—	
Tradition	.02	.13	.37	.16	-.30	.09	-.06	.04	.28	—

Note. AES - Aesthetics, AFF - Affiliation, ALT - Altruistic, CML - Commercial, HDN - Hedonistic, PWR - Power, REC - Recognition, SCI - Science, SEC - Security, TRA - Tradition.

Factor Structure

Table 2.6 presents a principal components analysis of the correlation matrix presented in Table 2.5. As seen, four components account for 67% of the variance in the matrix. The first component is defined by Recognition, Power, and Hedonistic and resembles Spranger's (1928) political attitude, Murray's (1938) achievement and dominance needs, and Holland's (1987) enterprising type. The second component is defined by Altruistic, Affiliation, and Tradition motives and corresponds to Spranger's social attitude, Murray's affiliation and nurturance needs, and Holland's social type. The third component is defined by Security and Commercial motives and corresponds to Spranger's economic attitude, Murray's acquisition and succorance needs, and Holland's conventional type. The final component, defined by Aesthetic and Scientific motives, corresponds to Spranger's aesthetic and theoretical attitudes, Murray's sentience and understanding needs, and Holland's artistic and investigative types. Because the MVPI is designed to cover historically significant and practically important motive themes, we made no attempt to develop scales that are statistically independent. The results in Tables 2.5 and 2.6 show the relations between the MVPI scales: they are sensible and interpretable.

Table 2.6

Principal Components Analysis for MVPI Scales

	Components			
	I	II	III	IV
Recognition	.78			
Power	.72			
Hedonistic	.66			
Altruistic		.82		
Affiliation	.45	.68		
Tradition		.62	.43	
Security			.77	
Commercial	.54		.61	
Aesthetic				.83
Scientific				.73

CHAPTER 3

VALIDITY

Construct Validity

The usefulness of a psychometric instrument depends on the appropriateness of decisions made from test score information. The critical problem for test users is to understand the meaning of test scores, which can be a complex process. We believe the best way to discover the meaning of a test score is to develop a theory regarding the latent structure underlying both test scores and criteria. The process of correlating scale scores with all other available measures is inefficient. Instead, using the theory of what the scale is supposed to measure, we can predict its relations (and lack of relations), and then use data to evaluate our hypotheses.

For the MVPI, the most important sources of validity information are item content and correlations between scale scores and other well-validated tests and observers' ratings. Investigating these relations in the context of ideas about what the scales are intended to measure is analogous to hypothesis testing. This process is construct validation and it relies on multiple sources of evidence to infer meaning from scale scores. Overall, the MVPI is a psychometrically sound assessment tool (Feltham & Loan-Clarke, 2007) with sufficient construct validity (Hogan, J., & Hogan, 1996).

Item Content

Like other interest measures, the MVPI items are content valid (Feltham & Loan-Clarke, 2007; Zedeck, 2001). The test items represent the motives, values, and interests that are being measured. Responses to the items provide a direct index of a person's feelings about the subject. For example, the answer to the item "In my spare time I would like to go to art museums or listen to classical music" directly reflects the respondent's aesthetic values and interests. Each MVPI scale was constructed to reflect five themes, and items were written to represent the expression of the motive construct through the theme. Consider the Aesthetic scale; the following items express the five themes: (a) Lifestyles - "I like to spend my free time reading novels and listening to classical music," (b) Beliefs - "A dedication to art is the highest calling in life," (c) Occupational Preferences - "I would like to be an artist or a musician," (d) Aversions - "I dislike being with people who have no interest in the arts," and (e) Preferred Associates - "I like to be around artists and writers."

These are examples of content valid items from the Aesthetic scale. Items on the remaining nine scales were constructed using the same content process. For each scale, the item was examined and compared with the intended content theme. Using this method of item construction, content validation is straightforward.

Correlations with Other Tests

Tables 3.1 through 3.7 present correlations between the MVPI scales and other well known psychological measures. These tables include four types of tests: measures of interests, normal personality, dysfunctional personality, and cognitive ability.

The Self-Directed Search (SDS; Holland, 1985b) is an interest inventory that assesses the six occupational types based on Holland's (1985a) theory of careers. The SDS is the most widely used interest inventory in the world. It is scored for six occupational types: (a) Realistic (R); (b) Investigative (I); (c) Artistic (A); (d) Social (S); (e) Enterprising (E); and (f) Conventional (C). A sample (N = 167) of male and female high school seniors provided the data for the SDS and the MVPI.

The measures of normal personality in the tables are the Myers-Briggs Type Indicator (MBTI; Myers & McCaulley, 1985) and the Hogan Personality Inventory (HPI; R. Hogan & J. Hogan, 1995; 2007). The MBTI is the most widely used personality inventory in modern America; it is designed to assess 16 types defined by Jungian theory (Jung, 1923). The types are composed of combinations of four basic mental functions: (a) sensing (S); (b) intuition (N); (c) thinking (T); and (d) feeling (F); two attitudes or orientations toward life: extraversion (E) and introversion (I); and two orientations to the outer world: judging (J) and perceiving (P). For research, preferences are expressed in continuous scores with lower scores indicating preferences for E, S, T, and J and higher scores indicating preferences for I, N, F, and P. A sample (N= 46) of male and female graduate students completed the MBTI and the MVPI.

The HPI is a 206-item inventory of normal personality based on the Big-Five personality dimensions. The HPI is used primarily in occupational settings for personnel selection, placement, coaching, and individualized assessment. The HPI contains seven primary scales and a validity scale. The primary scales and their Big-Five counterparts are: (a) Adjustment (Emotional Stability); (b) Ambition (Extraversion); (c) Sociability (Extraversion); (d) Interpersonal Sensitivity (Agreeableness); (e) Prudence (Conscientiousness); (f) Inquisitive (Intellect/Openness); and (g) Learning Approach (Intellect/Openness). A sample (N = 2,508) of male and female employed adults provided data for the HPI and the MVPI.

The measures of dysfunctional personality included the Minnesota Multiphasic Personality Inventory (MMPI; Hathaway & McKinley, 1943) and the Hogan Development Survey (HDS; R. Hogan & J. Hogan, 1997, 2009). The MMPI was designed to assess serious psychopathology and it (and the recent revision) is the most widely used test of psychopathology in the world. The MMPI includes three validity keys - Lie (L), Fake Bad (F), and Correction (K) - and 10 clinical scales: (a) Hypochondriasis (Hs); (b) Depression (D); (c) Hysteria (Hy); (d) Psychopathic Deviate (Pd); (e)

Masculinity-Feminin-ity (Mf); (e) Paranoia (Pa); (f) Psychasthenia (Pt); (g) Schizophrenia (Sc); (h) Hypomania (Ma); and (I) Social Introversion (Si). The sample (N = 134) who completed the MMPI and the MVPI were male and female police officer job applicants.

The HDS is a 168-item inventory to identify dysfunctional dispositions that may prevent a person from achieving full career potential. The scales were developed from and validated against employ-ment derailment factors. Although some of the personality constructs are similar to the DSM IV, Axis 2 personality disorders, there is no psychiatric stigma associated with scale scores; no inferences about mental disabilities can be made from the test results. The HDS contains one scale to detect socially desirable responding and 11 content scales: (a) Reserved; (b) Skeptical ; (c) Excitable; (d) Imaginative; (e) Colorful; (f) Bold; (g) Cautious; (h) Dutiful; (i) Leisurely; (j) Diligent; and (k) Mischievous. A sample (N = 140) of male and female sales and marketing employees completed the HDS and the MVPI.

The measures of cognitive ability presented in the tables are the Watson-Glaser Critical Thinking Appraisal (Watson & Glaser, 1980) and the Industrial Reading Test (Psychological Corporation, 1989). The Watson-Glaser is a widely used measure of critical thinking, composed of 80 items across five content areas. These include inference, recognition of assumptions, deduction, interpretation, and evaluation of arguments. For each area, stimulus passages are presented and several conclusions follow. The test taker examines each conclusion and makes decisions about its truth or falsity. Correct responses are summed for a total test score. The Industrial Reading Test is a power test of reading comprehension. It consists of nine reading passages and 38 items. Although the passages focus on work-relevant topics, performance does not depend on knowledge of industrial subject matter. Reading difficulty is reported to be high school level. A sample (N = 117) of male and female railroad applicants for service lane coordinator, yardmaster, dispatcher, and locomotive engineer jobs completed the Watson-Glaser and the MVPI; a sample (N= 83) male and female railroad applicants for service lane coordinator and dispatcher jobs completed the Industrial Reading Testing and the MVPI.

We discuss the MVPI correlational data for each inventory separately. The presentation is organized in terms of scale convergence and independence. The pattern of test correlates is one way to evaluate construct validity and to summarize inferences that can be made from the MVPI scale scores.

MVPI and the Self-Directed Search

We hypothesized that the largest correlations between the six SDS scales and the MVPI would be for SDS Investigative, Artistic, and Conventional scales. Because the SDS Social and Enterprising scales entail broader themes, we predicted their pattern of relations with the MVPI scales would be more diffuse. Finally, we judged that there would be no good counterpart of the SDS Realistic scale in the

MVPI. Table 3.1 shows the intercorrelations between the two inventories and as seen, the highest single relation is between the SDS Artistic scale and the MVPI Aesthetic scale (r = .66). This is followed by the correlation between SDS Conventional and MVPI Commercial scales (r = .51) and the correlation between SDS Investigative and MVPI Scientific scales (r = .47). As predicted, the SDS Enterprising scale correlated with MVPI scales of Commercial, Recognition, and Power at .51, .51, and .48, respectively. Similarly, the SDS Social scale was most closely associated with both the MVPI Altruism and Affiliation scales, r = .41 and .37, respectively. The MVPI scale that comes closest to representing the SDS Realistic construct is Scientific (r = .34).

Table 3.1

Correlations between the Self-Directed Search and the MVPI

Scale	Realistic	Investigative	Artistic	Social	Enterprising	Conventional
Aesthetic	-.12	.03	.66***	.34***	.13*	-.03
Affiliation	-.11	-.05	.15*	.37***	.35***	.07
Altruistic	-.08	.01	.26***	.41***	.13*	.12
Commercial	.15*	.16*	-.04	.13*	.51***	.51***
Hedonistic	-.05	.01	.05	.11	.20**	-.01
Power	.06	.18**	-.02	.19**	.48***	.26***
Recognition	.06	.09	.16*	.25***	.51***	.20**
Scientific	.34***	.47***	-.09	-.10	.18**	.00
Security	.01	.03	-.10	.01	.02	.15*
Tradition	.03	-.06	.14*	.17*	.11	.02

Note. N = 167; *p < .10; ** p < .05; *** p < .01

Note that the MVPI Hedonistic, Security, and Tradition scales have no strong counterparts on the SDS. In addition, the "people" scales of the MVPI - Aesthetic, Affiliation, and Altruistic - have a negative manifold with the "technical things" Realistic scale of the SDS. The same pattern of relations seen in Holland's hexagon display of the SDS scales appears when the MVPI marker scales are placed in the same geometric arrangement. Finally, the correlations between SDS and MVPI scales that were predicted to be independent are either low or non-significant.

MVPI and the Myers-Briggs Type Indicator

We hypothesized that the MBTI EI scale should be highly correlated with the MVPI Affiliation scale and the SN scale should be highly positively correlated with the MVPI Aesthetic scale, and negatively correlated with the Security scale. The remaining two MBTI scales (TF and JP) are poorly defined and their interpretations are not well supported by data. Therefore, it is difficult to hypothesize relations between the TF and JP scales and the MVPI scales.

Table 3.2 shows the correlations between the four MBTI scales and the ten scales of the MVPI. As seen, the highest correlation is between EI and the MVPI Affiliation scale (r = -.71), suggesting that the Affiliation scale is a good marker for EI. Also, strong correlations are seen between SN and the

MVPI Aesthetic and Security scales in the hypothesized direction (r = .61 and -.68, respectively). These two MVPI scales appear to be good construct representatives for the SN scale because they concern creativity - Aesthetic motives entail a preference for creative self-expression and Security motives entail a preference for the concrete and the certain. The MBTI TF scale is correlated positively with the MVPI Altruistic (r = .40) and negatively with the Power (r = -.34) and Scientific (r = -.36) scales. The MBTI JP scale is correlated positively with Aesthetic (r = .29) and negatively with Security (r = -.40) and Tradition (r = -.40).

Table 3.2

Correlations between the Myers-Briggs Type Indicator and the MVPI

Scale	EI	SN	TF	JP
Aesthetic	.21	.61***	.16	.29*
Affiliation	-.71***	-.10	.28	.10
Altruistic	-.29	-.11	.40**	.00
Commercial	-.21	-.30*	-.09	-.02
Hedonistic	-.15	.08	-.01	.28
Power	-.19	.02	-.34*	.02
Recognition	-.12	.19	-.03	.25
Scientific	.10	.24	-.36*	.19
Security	.00	-.68***	.09	-.40**
Tradition	-.39**	-.35*	-.09	-.40**

Note. N = 46; EI=Extraversion-Introversion, SN=Sensing-Intuition, TF=Thinking-Feeling, JP=Judging-Perceiving; * p < .05; ** p < .01; *** p < .001, one-tailed test.

The first two scales of the MBTI are well represented by MVPI variables. Affiliation is a good proxy for EI and the combination of Aesthetic and Security are good proxies for SN. However, the other MBTI-MVPI correlations may tell us more about the MBTI TF and JP scales than vice versa. High TF is associated with values for serving society and the less fortunate (+ Altruistic), lack of interest in competition, achievement, and personal advancement (- Power), and greater use of intuition than analysis (- Scientific). High JP is associated with values for the creative and needs for self-expression (+ Aesthetic), preferences for risk taking and testing the limits (- Security), and desire for novelty, experimentation, and innovation (- Tradition).

MVPI and the Hogan Personality Inventory

We hypothesized that all of the MVPI scales would be significantly related to Big-Five personality factors. We predicted that some scales would be saturated with more than one Big-Five construct whereas others would be clearly marked by a single personality factor. In addition, we anticipated some negative relations between personality and motive scales. Table 3.3 presents the results.

Table 3.3

Correlations between the Hogan Personality Inventory and the MVPI

	Adjustment	Ambition	Sociability	Interpersonal Sensitivity	Prudence	Inquisitive	Learning Approach
Aesthetic	-.20***	-.05**	.23***	-.01	-.18***	.39***	.17***
Affiliation	.28***	.36***	.41***	.38***	.15***	.15***	.08***
Altruistic	.10***	.08***	.03	.26***	.23***	.12***	.04*
Commercial	.11***	.25***	.21***	.13***	.18***	.19***	.16***
Hedonistic	-.34***	-.16***	.33***	-.02	-.39***	.07***	-.08***
Power	.05**	.37***	.36***	.06***	.01	.26***	.20***
Recognition	-.18***	.11***	.51***	.01	-.19***	.23***	.06**
Scientific	-.09***	-.04**	.05**	-.02	-.04*	.27***	.11***
Security	.02	-.09***	-.28***	.03	.34***	-.20***	-.11***
Tradition	.20***	.18***	-.10***	.11***	.34***	.04*	.08***

Note. N = 2,508; * p < .05; ** p < .01; *** p < .001, one-tailed test.

The Aesthetic scale is positively correlated with the HPI Inquisitive scale (r = .39) and negatively correlated with the Adjustment scale (r = -.20). This negative correlation is consistent with Barron's (1965) data for various creative samples. Affiliation is correlated with all the HPI scales and the strongest relations are with HPI scales concerning interpersonal dispositions - Sociability, Interpersonal Sensitivity, and Ambition. Altruistic is correlated with the agreeable and conscientiousness dimensions of the HPI (Interpersonal Sensitivity r = .26; Prudence r = .23). The Commercial and Power scales have their highest correlations with the HPI Ambition scale (r = .25 and .37, respectively). As expected, Hedonistic is negatively related to HPI Prudence (r = -.39), while Prudence is positively related to Security (r = .34) and Tradition (r = .34). Recognition and Scientific are associated with a single personality construct; Recognition correlated .51 with HPI Sociability, and Scientific correlated .27 with HPI Inquisitive.

MVPI and the Minnesota Multiphasic Personality Inventory

We hypothesized that about half of the MVPI scales would have significant correlates with MMPI scales and we judged that the scale to scale relations would entail specific constructs and not multiple or generalized personality dysfunctions. However, we predicted that the MMPI Hypomania (Ma) scale would have a greater number of positive MVPI correlates than any of the other scales because Ma involves high energy and self-confidence. Table 3.4 presents the results.

Table 3.4

Correlations between the Minnesota Multiphasic Personality Inventory and the MVPI

	L	F	K	Hs	D	Hy	Pd
AES	-.01	.05	-.12	-.03	.07	-.10	.01
AFF	.05	-.11	.17*	.08	.07	.27**	-.12
ALT	.14	-.12	.04	.01	.02	-.01	-.07
CML	.18*	.05	.02	-.12	.01	-.04	-.02
HDN	-.12	.16*	-.34**	.08	-.05	-.24**	-.03
PWR	.00	.02	-.19*	.01	-.08	-.13	.03
REC	-.21**	.10	-.31**	.12	-.08	-.26**	.13
SCI	.10	-.09	.07	-.21**	.18*	-.02	-.11
SEC	.16*	-.11	-.03	-.01	-.08	-.24**	-.21**
TRA	.31**	.01	.16*	-.10	-.05	.01	-.08

	Mf	Pa	Pt	Sc	Ma	Si	
AES	.30**	.13	.18*	.09	.25**	-.12	
AFF	-.08	.14	-.13	-.02	.11	-.48**	
ALT	.06	.03	.15*	-.02	.20**	.06	
CML	-.03	.07	-.08	-.01	.15*	-.10	
HDN	-.12	-.12	.22**	.25**	.32**	-.19*	
PWR	-.06	-.01	.09	.05	.33**	-.09	
REC	-.04	.03	.28**	.29**	.41**	-.21**	
SCI	-.16*	.03	-.15*	-.19*	.01	-.22**	
SEC	-.25**	-.24**	-.09	-.20**	.06	.12	
TRA	-.04	-.08	-.04	-.13	-.04	.18*	

Note. N = 134; L = Lie, F = Fake Bad, K = Correction, Hs = Hypochondriasis, D = Depression, Hy = Hysteria, Pd = Psychopathic Deviate, Mf = Masculinity-Femininity, Pa = Paranoia, Pt = Psychasthenia, Sc = Schizophrenia, Ma = Hypomania, Si = Social Introversion; AES = Aesthetic, AFF = Affiliation, ALT = Altruistic, CML = Commercial, HDN = Hedonism, PWR = Power, REC = Recognition, SCI = Science, SEC = Security, TRA = Tradition; $* p < .05$; $** p < .01$, one-tailed test.

Consistent with Barron's (1965) findings with creative samples, the Aesthetic scale is significantly related to MMPI Mf (r = .30); persons with high Mf scores are described as interpersonally sensitive and interested in intellectual or artistic activities. Affiliation is positively related to MMPI Hy (r = .27); high scores on Hy are interpreted as concern with social image and presenting self in an overly favorable way. Hedonistic is positively related to MMPI Ma (r = .32) and negatively related to MMPI K (r = -.34); this pattern suggests that the Hedonistic scale captures social, outgoing, and impulsive behavior as well as overindulgence, carelessness, and risk taking. In addition, higher Hedonistic scores reflect a willingness to be open, frank, and disclosing. Both Power and Recognition scales are associated with MMPI Ma (r = .33 and .41, respectively) which reflects initiative, energy, and apparent self-confidence. The Recognition scale correlates with MMPI Sc and Pt (r = .29 and .28, respectively) suggesting that the need for Recognition is driven by low self-confidence and feelings of inadequacy. Finally, the Tradition scale has its highest correlation with the MMPI L scale (r = .31), indicating that high scores on Tradition are self-conscientiously virtuous and reluctant to admit common faults - clergymen as a group receive high scores on the MMPI L scale.

The Altruistic, Commercial, Scientific, and Security scales have no particular interpretable correlations with the MMPI.

MVPI and the Hogan Development Survey

We hypothesized a number of relations between the motive scales and dysfunctional personality characteristics. This may seem counterintuitive because motives are desires and preferences, not personality characteristics. Nonetheless, we believe that some motive patterns should covary positively with negative personality characteristics (e.g., Power and Bold) while others should covary negatively (e.g., Affiliation and Reserved). In terms of positive covariation, we predicted that Aesthetic, Commercial, Hedonistic, Power, Recognition, and Security would be associated with some dysfunctional personality characteristics. In terms of negative covariation, we predicted that Affiliation, Altruism, Scientific, and Tradition would be associated with the absence of personality dysfunction. The results appear in Table 3.5.

Table 3.5

Correlations between the Hogan Development Survey and the MVPI

	RES	EXC	CAU	IMA	DUT	SKE	LEI	COL	BOL	DIL	MIS
AES	.07	.06	.09	.33**	-.02	.01	.01	.20**	.17*	-.02	.16*
AFF	-.64**	-.46**	-.48**	.23**	-.09	.04	-.19**	.46**	.31**	.04	.34**
ALT	-.25**	-.02	.17*	.04	.38**	-.04	.08	-.08	.02	.21**	-.03
CML	-.05	.02	-.19**	.14	-.13	.28**	.22**	.16*	.50**	.25**	.29**
HDN	-.06	.07	.08	.15*	.10	.28**	.13	.15*	.11	.13	.21**
PWR	-.14*	-.06	-.33**	.37**	-.21**	.32**	.20**	.46**	.68**	.18*	.54**
REC	-.05	.01	-.23**	.42**	-.21**	.24**	.10	.58**	.68**	-.07	.52**
SCI	-.08	-.01	-.11	.21**	-.15*	.03	.09	.09	.23**	.11	.10
SEC	.06	.14*	.35**	-.39**	.37**	.02	.20**	-.43**	-.06	.41**	-.38**
TRA	-.08	.13	.12	.04	.30**	.06	.09	-.11	.02	.30**	-.06

Note. N = 140; RES = Reserved, EXC = Excitable, CAU = Cautious, IMA = Imaginative, DUT = Dutiful, SKE = Skeptical, LEI = Leisurely, COL = Colorful, BOL = Bold, DIL = Diligent, MIS = Mischievous; AES = Aesthetic, AFF = Affiliation, ALT = Altruistic, CML = Commercial, HDN = Hedonism, PWR = Power, REC = Recognition, SCI = Science, SEC = Security, TRA = Tradition; * p < .05; ** p < .01; one-tailed test.

The Power scale has more correlations with personality dysfunctions than any other MVPI scale. These include the HDS scales for Imaginative (r = .37), Skeptical (r = .32), Colorful (r = .46), Bold (r = .68), and Mischievous (r = .54). In addition, Power is negatively related to the HDS Cautious scale (r = -.33). Higher scores on the Power motive reflect charisma and energy, willingness to compete and to test the limits, attention seeking, and high self-confidence. The pattern of correlates is similar for the Recognition motive, with positive relations for the HDS Imaginative, Colorful, Bold, and Mischievous scales (r's = .42, .58, .68, and .52, respectively).

The Security motive is correlated with both positive and negative dysfunctional dispositions. There are positive relations with the HDS Cautious, Dutiful, and Diligent scales (r's = .35, .37, and .41, respectively) and negative relations with the HDS Imaginative and Colorful scales (r's = -.39 and -.43, respectively). Higher scores on the Security motive reflect fearfulness and self-doubt, need for support and advice from others, and conscientiousness and attention to detail. In addition, high scorers are characterized as predictable, consistent, reserved, and lacking leadership skills. Similarly, the Affiliation scale has positive and negative correlations with dysfunctional dispositions. The HDS triad that reflects need for attention, energy, and social skill - Colorful, Bold, and Mischievous - are positively related (r's = .46, .31, and .34, respectively) to Affiliation. The HDS triad that reflects social ineptness and inappropriate affect - Reserved, Excitable, and Cautious - are negatively correlated (r's = -.64, -.46, and -.48, respectively) with Affiliation.

As predicted, some motives are associated with narrowly focused dysfunctional dispositions. For example, the Aesthetic scale is correlated with the HDS Imaginative scale (r = .33). Both Altruism and the Tradition motives are correlated with the HDS Dutiful scale (r's = .38 and .30, respectively), indicating eagerness to please. The Commercial scale is correlated with HDS Bold (r = .50). Finally, neither the Hedonistic scale nor the Scientific scale is strongly related to any of the dysfunctional dispositions measured by the HDS.

MVPI and Cognitive Measures

We hypothesized that with the exceptions of the MVPI Aesthetic and Scientific scales, the remaining scales would be unrelated to cognitive ability. Both the Aesthetic and Scientific scales contain some item content that could reflect academic and intellectual interests; the underlying analytic ability would account for the correlation between motives and cognitive performance. Table 3.6 shows the correlations between the Watson-Glaser and the MVPI scales. Only one predicted relation emerged. The correlation between the Aesthetic scale and the Watson-Glaser was significant (r = .17), while the correlation with Scientific was not. The Watson-Glaser was positively related to Recognition (r = .18) and negatively related to Security (r = -.30) and Altruistic (r = -.19). Presenting the results from the Industrial Reading Test, Table 3.7 shows that only the correlation between Aesthetic and reading comprehension was significant (r = .18). Together, these results indicate that cognitive ability, as measured by tests used frequently in business and industry, is related to Aesthetic motives and unrelated to the other nine.

Table 3.6

Correlations between the Watson-Glaser Critical Thinking Appraisal and the MVPI

	AES	AFF	ALT	COM	HED	POW	REC	SCI	SEC	TRA
Watson-Glaser	.17*	.04	-.19*	.10	.15	.12	.18*	.00	-.30**	-.09

Note. N = 117; AES = Aesthetic; AFF = Affiliation; ALT = Altruistic; COM = Commercial; HED = Hedonistic; POW = Power; REC = Recognition; SCI = Scientific; SEC = Security; TRA = Tradition; * p < .05; ** p < .01; one-tailed test.

Table 3.7

Correlations between the Industrial Reading Test and the MVPI

	AES	AFF	ALT	COM	HED	POW	REC	SCI	SEC	TRA
Industrial Reading Test	.18*	.00	.02	.15	.07	.06	.11	.10	-.15	.02

Note. N = 83; AES = Aesthetic; AFF = Affiliation; ALT = Altruistic; COM = Commercial; HED = Hedonistic; POW = Power; REC = Recognition; SCI = Scientific; SEC = Security; TRA = Tradition; * $p < .05$; ** $p < .01$; one-tailed test.

Correlations with Others' Descriptions

Although test validity is at the heart of test usage, the concept is often poorly understood. The validity of a measure is often defined in practice in terms of its correlations with a few other measures and inventories chosen on the basis of sheer convenience. Some of the results in the previous section are examples of this. In our view, however, a more adequate definition of validity concerns the number of empirically supported inferences about real world performance that we can make about a test score. By far the most useful inferences concern how others will describe people with high and low scores on a particular measure. Thus, we consider correlations between scale scores and observer descriptions to be essential validity information.

Because the MVPI is useful for individualized assessment, employee development, and understanding how to manage/reward others, we also view correlations between scale scores and others' descriptions as a major source of interpretive information. We want to know whether MVPI scores are reliably correlated with observer descriptions. We also want to know about the degree to which descriptions are consistent across observers at different organizational levels (e.g., subordinates, peers, and bosses). We gathered MVPI scores and observer descriptions for six samples in two organizations. People completed the MVPI while at work and anonymous observers described them using a checklist.

The first set of results is based on subordinates' (N = 500) descriptions of their managers (N = 99) in a large metropolitan hospital in the southwest. These results are labeled "Subordinate" in Table 3.8. The second set of results is peers' (N = 200) ratings of managers (N = 74) at the same hospital. Managers completed the MVPI and observers evaluated them for 55 descriptive phrases using a 5-point rating scale where "5" indicated strongly agree and "1" indicated strongly disagree. The 55 descriptive phrases were developed from behaviors known to be associated with effective and ineffective organizational performance. These results are labeled "Peer" in Table 3.8. The third set of results is based on bosses' (N = 35) descriptions of subordinates (N = 155) in a large transportation company in the southeast. Subordinates completed the MVPI and bosses evaluated them using a 200 item checklist where "Y" indicated characteristic of the subordinate, "U" indicated unsure, and "N" indicated not characteristic of the subordinate. The content of this checklist was unique in that it contained work-related behavioral items, Big-Five adjectival descriptors (Goldberg, 1992), and terms describing the 10 personality disorders (American Psychiatric Association, 1994). Inclusion of personality disorder descriptors restores an evaluative component to the emotionally homogenized "non-evaluative" trait lists typically used in personality research (cf. John, 1990). These results are labeled "Boss" in Table 3.8.

Correlations between observers' ratings across three organizational levels and MVPI scores appear in Table 3.8. The correlations between Aesthetic motives and subordinates' and peers' descriptions reflect, on the one hand, flexibility, assigning work to develop new skills, and having good working relations with customers. On the other hand, high scorers for Aesthetic motives are seen by their bosses as flighty, quick to anger, easily bored, nonconforming, and disorganized.

The pattern of correlations between Affiliation scores and peer descriptions reflect frequent communication, willingness to share credit, and willingness to provide constructive feedback. Subordinates describe these high scoring managers as not projecting a clear vision and not listening to the workforce. Bosses see high Affiliation subordinates as trusting, kind, conforming, comfortable meeting new people, and also encouraging constructive feedback. Consequently, peers and bosses regard high Affiliation scores in positive terms - social, considerate, communicative, and conforming; subordinates of high Affiliation bosses, however, see a person who is disorganized, won't confront problem employees, and talks, but won't listen.

The pattern of correlations for the Altruistic scale reflects concern for the well being of the work group. Peers and bosses describe high scorers as conducting organized meetings, keeping others informed, fostering communication as well as being sympathetic, responding to advice, and having good common sense. High scorers are also seen as unassertive, unable to balance personal and work life, and frequently late for scheduled events.

The pattern of correlations between the Commercial scale and ratings reflects fairly consistent descriptions across observer group, but the description is not particularly flattering. Persons with high scores on the Commercial scale are seen by others as difficult, selfish, and tough. Although not charming, such characteristics are useful when interactions involve negotiations, agenda setting, and holding people accountable.

The pattern of correlations for Hedonistic scores and subordinates' ratings indicate that high scorers are seen as calm under pressure, even-tempered, and striking a balance between work and family. Peers rate persons with high scores for Hedonistic as failing to deliver on promises and failing to recognize their own strengths and weaknesses. Bosses see Hedonistic subordinates as flirtatious, the life of the office, dramatic, and prone to engage in horseplay.

The pattern of correlations for Power scores and subordinates' and bosses' ratings are fairly consistent. They describe persons with high scores for Power as leaders - not followers, aggressive, pushing the limits, accepting challenge, working hard, and having a vision. Peers, on the other hand, describe their high Power scoring peers as bossy and pushy ("Won't allow us to make our own decisions"), arrogant ("Won't share credit with us"), and indifferent ("Doesn't show genuine interest in me"). These descriptors demonstrate how the achievement behavior of power oriented people is viewed by different constituencies in the organization.

The pattern of correlations for Recognition motives varies by observer group. Subordinates describe high scoring bosses as not sharing credit, not taking responsibility for mistakes, and not trustworthy. Peers describe high scoring peers as sharing developmental opportunities, doing a good job in meetings, and meeting objectives. Bosses describe high scoring subordinates as attracting the attention of others ("Engages in horseplay"), encouraging conflict, and not being a good follower.

The pattern of correlations for the Scientific scale suggests that high scorers value innovation and technical developments, are efficient and organized, and become easily bored.

The pattern of correlations for the Security scale reflects concern for conformity, seriousness, rigidity and lack of leadership skills. Bosses describe subordinates with high Security scores, on the one hand, as socially appropriate, quiet, and restrained and, on the other hand, as fearing performance appraisal and working best alone, as a follower, and as avoiding social encounters.

The observer descriptions for the Tradition scale come almost exclusively from bosses' ratings of subordinates. In this sample, bosses described persons with high scores for Tradition as responding to advice from superiors, having good common sense, and as trusting. They are also described as not flirtatious, as not likely to examine alternative courses of action, and as having odd attitudes. Curiously, there were no significant peer correlates of peer Tradition scale scores. Finally, the highest correlation ($r = -.32$) across the observer groups was negative and between subordinates' ratings for the item "I am proud to be part of this team" and bosses' Tradition scale scores. This seems to reflect how subordinates react to bosses who are overly concerned with procedures and ensuring that everyone follows the rules. This captures the morale depressing effect of micromanagement.

Table 3.8

Correlations between Observers' Description Ratings and the MVPI

MVPI Scale	Observers Description Item	Observer		
		Subordinate	Peer	Boss
Aesthetic	Assigns work that helps us learn new skills	.18**		
	Controls temper in front of customers and staff	.20**		
	Is flexible in uncertain situations	.13*		
	Customers like working with my peer		.23**	
	Peer is able to coordinate people who need to work together		.18*	
	Tends to be flighty			.20**
	Tends to be nonconforming			.17*
	Is organized			-.17*
	Is quick to become angry			.19*
	Is easily bored			.22*
Affiliation	Acts quickly and fairly when dealing with problem staff members	-.16*		
	Listens to me when I have something important to say	-.17*		
	Has a clear vision of where we are going as a team	-.20**		
	Shares credit with all of us when we do something upper management likes		.24**	
	Keeps staff informed about developments in the company		.26**	
	Takes time to discuss how the team is working together		.28**	
	Offers constructive feedback		.23**	
	Shares positive feedback with me which makes me feel valued		.23	
	Is trusting			.24**
	Enjoys meeting new people			.26**
	Tends to be nonconforming			-.17*
	Encourages constructive criticism			.19**
	Is Kind			.22**
Altruistic	Fosters open communication	.16*		
	Responds quickly to requests	.17*		
	Keeps staff informed about developments in company	.22**		
	Maintains proper balance between personal and work life		-.37***	
	Is on time for work, appointments, and meetings		-.29***	
	Conducts meetings in well organized way		.23**	
	Is assertive			-.17*
	Is sympathetic			.18-
	Has good common sense			.17*
	Responds to advice			.17*
Validity				

Table 3.8

Correlations between Observers' Description Ratings and the MVPI (Continued)

MVPI Scale	Observers Description Item		Observer	
		Subordinate	Peer	Boss
Commercial	Customers like working with my supervisor	-.25***		
	Controls temper in front of staff and customers	-.20**		
	Is calm when working under pressure	-.20**		
	Shares credit with us when we do something upper management really likes		-.26**	
	Listens to me when I have something important to say		-.24**	
	Easy for my peer to work with a variety of people		-.22**	
	I am hesitant to disagree with my peer		.25*	
	Places team objectives above personal goals			-.21**
	Tends to be nonconforming			.21**
	Is easy going			-.24**
	Is socially inept			-.21**
	Is the life of the office			-.25**
	Is practical			.18*
Hedonistic	Controls temper in front of customers and staff	.15*		
	Is calm when working under pressure	.18**		
	Does what is promised when it is promised		-.23**	
	Knows strengths and areas to improve		-.20**	
	Tends to be dramatic			.17*
	Is flirtatious			.33**
	Is the life of the office			.21**
	Engages in horseplay			.21**
Power	Accepts difficult challenges	.16*		
	Works hard for the company	.15*		
	Has a clear vision of where we are going as a team	.21**		
	Shares credit with us when we do something upper management really likes		-.18*	
	Shows a genuine interest in me and understands when I need help		-.17*	
	Allows us to make our own decisions		-.27*	
	Is assertive			.18*
	Is a follower			-.27**
	Is self-restrained			-.21**
	Lacks leadership skills			-.20**
	Tests the limits			.23**

34   Validity

Table 3.8

Correlations between Observers' Description Ratings and the MVPI (Continued)

MVPI Scale	Observers Description Item		Observer	
		Subordinate	Peer	Boss
Recognition	Shares credit with us when we do something upper management really likes	-.18**		
	Does what is promised when it is promised	-.14*		
	Takes responsibility for mistakes	-.16*		
	Represents staff concerns accurately to upper management		.21*	
	Conducts meetings in a well organized way		.26**	
	Meets team objectives		.23**	
	Shares training and developmental activities (n = 39)		.30**	
	Is a follower			-.18*
	Engages in horseplay			.34**
	Encourages conflict			.19*
Scientific	Places team objectives above personal goals	.18**		
	Accepts difficult challenges	.19**		
	Follows company rules and procedures	.23**		
	Is on top of new technical and business information		.36***	
	Conducts meetings in a well organized way (n = 45)		.25**	
	Is empathetic			-.19*
	Is kind			.22**
	Is quick to become angry			.22**
	Lacks leadership skills			-.14*
	Is easily bored			.21**
Security	Is patient and considerate even when the work load is heavy	-.20**		
	Is on time for work, appointments, and meetings	.19**		
	Follows company rules and procedures	.19**		
	Allows us to make our own decisions	-.20**		
	Acts quickly and fairly when dealing with problem staff members		.17*	
	Is able to coordinate people who need to work together		-.20**	
	Easy for my peer to work with a variety of people		-.25**	
	Is on time for work, appointments, and meetings		.20**	
	Avoids social encounters			.18*
	Is a follower			.20**
	Is quiet			.22**
	Is self-restrained			.21**
	Fears performance appraisals			.21**
	Works well alone			.19*
	Acts in a socially appropriate manner			.21*

Validity

Table 3.8

Correlations between Observers' Description Ratings and the MVPI (Continued)

MVPI Scale	Observers Description Item	Observer		
		Subordinate	Peer	Boss
Tradition	I am proud to be a part of this team	-.32***		
	Is trusting			.15*
	Tends to be suspicious			-.23**
	Fails to examine alternative courses of action			.18*
	Has good common sense			.26**
	Responds to advice			.27**
	Is flirtatious			-.20**
	Has odd attitudes			.20*

Note. * p < .10 ** p < .05 *** p < .01, one-tailed test.

CHAPTER 4

INTERPRETATIONS AND USES

General Interpretation

The scales on the MVPI are a reasonable sample of the range of human motives identified during 80 years of academic research (Hogan, J., & Hogan, 1996). Values, preferences, and interests are all motivational concepts; they differ primarily in terms of their generality - values are the broadest and most abstract kind of motive, and interests are the narrowest and most concrete kind of motive. These motivational concepts tell us about a person's desires and plans, and they explain the long-term themes and tendencies in a person's life.

There are two ways this motivational information can be useful. First, it can be used to evaluate the fit between a person's interests and the psychological requirements of jobs; thus, the MVPI can be used to help people choose occupations or careers. Second, the inventory can be used to evaluate the fit between a person's values and the climate of a particular organization; thus, the MVPI can be used to help people think strategically about their current careers.

Measures of motives, values, and interests are somewhat different from personality measures. Personality measures tell us what a person may do in certain situations, whereas value and interest inventories tell us what a person wants to do. Moreover, people tend not to distort their answers on interest measures because their values and aspirations are part of their identity and they are normally eager to discuss them. Finally, motives, values, and preferences are remarkably stable; they tend to change very little as a person grows older - what interests you now will probably interest you later.

The next section defines the scales on the MVPI and provides three levels of interpretation. These interpretations define high scores in terms of percentiles above 65 and low scores in terms of percentiles below 35. Hogan and Blake (1996) regard needs, values, and interests as closely related concepts. Distinguishing among them seems to be a matter of semantics and personal choice because the terms have been used interchangeably in much of psychology. Although values are often seen as the most inclusive construct, Dawis (1980) notes that, depending on the author, values are equated with beliefs (Allport, 1961; Rokeach, 1973), attitudes (Campbell, 1963), needs (Maslow, 1954), interests (Allport, 1961; Perry, 1954), and preferences (Katzell, 1964; Rokeach, 1973). Further interpretation of each scale is provided in the Hogan Guide (Hogan, Hogan, & Warrenfeltz, 2007).

Scale by Scale Interpretation

Aesthetic

Aesthetic motives are associated with being interested in art, literature, and music, and a lifestyle guided by issues of imagination, culture, and good taste. Persons with high scores on this scale care about aesthetic values and creative self-expression, and they tend to choose careers in art, music, advertising, journalism, or the entertainment industry. They tend to be independent, bright, original, and artistic, but also colorful, nonconforming, and impatient. People with low scores tend to be described as slow to anger, practical, and orderly.

If a person receives a *high* score on the Aesthetic scale, this suggests he is interested in artistic and cultural subjects; he is imaginative and potentially creative; and he will do his best work in environments that allow experimentation, exploration, and creativity. As a manager, he will enjoy innovation and he will care about the appearance of work products, but he may tend to be unpredictable or disorganized, and will prefer to solve problems on his own. People with high scores on this scale are often described by others as unpredictable, easily bored, and testing the limits.

If a person receives an *average* score on the Aesthetic scale, this suggests he has some artistic interests and values, but they are not dominant factors in his life. He is more likely concerned about the content than the appearance of work products.

If a person receives a *low* score on the Aesthetic scale, this suggests he is unconcerned with aesthetic values or artistic self-expression, and that he has practical interests and a business-like style. As a manager, he will tend to be stable, predictable, and willing to follow company policy; he should also be unconcerned with issues of personal autonomy or the appearance of work products. Finally, he will tend to be uninterested in innovation, possibly even resisting it.

Affiliation

Affiliative motives are associated with a need for frequent social contact and a lifestyle organized around social interaction. Persons with high scores on this scale tend to be outgoing, charming, and socially insightful, but somewhat conforming and possibly disorganized; they tend to choose careers that allow them plenty of contact with other people. Such careers include sales, supervision, mail carrier, health technician, or bartender. People with low scores on this scale tend to be described as shy, wary, and reluctant to confide in others.

If a person receives a *high* score on the Affiliation scale, this suggests she is adaptable, friendly, spontaneous, and outgoing, that she enjoys working with the public and dislikes working by herself. As a manager, she will tend to be kind, trusting, approachable, and a good corporate citizen, but perhaps somewhat dependent on the approval of upper management. People with high scores on this scale are often described as readily following company policy, and as being adaptable and open to criticism.

If a person receives an *average* score on the Affiliation scale, this suggests she has no strong preferences about working alone or with others. Unlike some people, she doesn't need to be with others; socializing with friends and colleagues is not her primary motivator.

If a person receives a *low* score on the Affiliation scale, this suggests she doesn't need constant or rapidly changing social contact; she may be somewhat shy, perhaps even suspicious about others' motives and not overly concerned with social approval; she enjoys working by herself and may not want to work in a team. As a manager, she will tend to be quiet and self-restrained, but independent and possibly not deeply concerned with pleasing senior management.

Altruistic

Altruistic motives are associated with a desire to serve others, improve society, help the less fortunate, and a lifestyle organized around making the world a better place to live. People with high scores on this scale care deeply about social justice, the plight of the have-nots, and the fate of the environment. They tend to be sensitive, sympathetic, unassertive, kindly, and choose careers in teaching, social work, counseling, and human resources. People with low scores on this scale tend to be described as good organizational citizens, but as not delegating readily or keeping others well informed.

If a person receives a *high* score on the Altruistic scale, this suggests he is likeable, responsible, idealistic, and good-natured. As a manager, he will listen well and be sensitive to staff and client needs, but may not be very forceful. He will enjoy helping others - including his subordinates to enhance their careers. Such people tend to be described as unassertive, sympathetic, and considerate.

If a person receives an *average* score on the Altruistic scale, this suggests that although he enjoys helping others, he probably won't devote his life to public service or spend time doing volunteer work for charitable organizations. He is more likely to contribute money than time to help others.

If a person receives a *low* score on the Altruistic scale, this suggests he doesn't endorse altruistic values, tends not to be interested in helping the less fortunate citizens of society, and may be assertive, forceful, forthright, and willing to confront people problems. As a manager, he will most likely be direct, and perhaps more interested in productivity than staff morale and development.

Commercial

Commercial motives are associated with an interest in earning money, realizing profits, finding business opportunities, and a lifestyle organized around investments and financial planning. Persons with high scores on this scale care deeply about monetary matters, material success, and income as a form of self-evaluation. They tend to be hard working, planful, organized, practical, and mature, and they tend to be financial or market analysts, bankers, accountants, real estate traders and developers, and stock brokers. People with low scores on this scale are more likely to be described as pleasant, empathic, and laid back.

If a person receives a *high* score on the Commercial scale, this suggests she is motivated by the prospects of financial gain, is serious about work, attentive to details, and comfortable working within specified guidelines. As a manager, she will most likely be businesslike, direct, and focused on the bottom line. People with high scores on this scale tend to be described as task-oriented, socially adroit, and serious.

If a person receives an *average* score on the Commercial scale, this suggests she is not indifferent to financial considerations, but neither is she preoccupied with them. Money will not be a major motivator in her life. At work, other priorities will interest her more than compensation.

If a person receives a *low* score on the Commercial scale, this suggests she is indifferent to Commercial values and tends to be easy-going, impractical, and unconcerned about material success. She will most likely not spend her spare time reading about or working on finance-related issues. As a manager, she will be sympathetic, relaxed, and loyal to her subordinates.

Hedonistic

Hedonistic motives are associated with a desire for pleasure, excitement, variety, and a lifestyle organized around good food, good drinks, entertaining friends, and fun times. Ideal occupations include restaurant critic, travel reviewer, convention site selector, wine taster, or race car driver (i.e., any occupation that involves entertainment and recreation). People with high scores on this scale like to play, tease, and entertain others. They tend to be dramatic, flirtatious, impulsive, and the life of the party. Persons with low scores tend to be quiet, unassertive, and predictable.

If a person receives a *high* score on the Hedonistic scale, this suggests he is expressive, playful, and changeable, and will prefer to work in a dynamic and fluid environment. As a manager, he will be colorful and entertaining, but unconcerned with details and may not learn from his mistakes. People with high scores on this scale also tend to be described as lively, fun-loving, and jolly, and have a well-developed capacity for enjoyment.

If a person receives an *average* score on the Hedonistic scale, this suggests that, although he likes to have a good time, he will usually put business before pleasure. He has a normal appetite for socializing and rarely engages in excess. He won't spend much time daydreaming about his next vacation.

If a person receives a *low* score on the Hedonistic scale, this suggests he tends to be self-disciplined, formal, reserved, and careful about what he says or does. As a manager he will be alert and concerned about details; he may also seem reluctant to relax and have a good time, especially when there is work to be done.

Power

Power motives are associated with a desire for challenge, competition, and achievement. Persons with high scores on this scale care deeply about being successful, getting ahead, and getting things done. They tend to be assertive, confident, and active, but also independent and willing to challenge authority. Although high scores for Power are associated with success in any occupation, they are especially important for careers in management, politics, and sales. People with low scores tend to be described as unassertive, socially inhibited, and cooperative.

If a person receives a *high* score on the Power scale, this suggests she is competitive, achievement-oriented, ambitious, and strategic about her career. As a manager, she will tend to be energetic, visionary, leaderlike, controlling, and willing to disagree with her superiors. People with high scores will likely be described as having leadership skills, challenging limits, and socially competent. They are most happy working in organizations where there are opportunities for upward mobility, and will tend to leave when such opportunities don't exist.

If a person receives an *average* score on the Power scale, this suggests that, although she takes pride in her achievements, there is also more to her life than her job. She is also willing to listen and let others describe her accomplishments. Although normally cooperative, she will take a stand if she feels strongly about an issue.

If a person receives a *low* score on the Power scale, this suggests she is uninterested in competition, achievement, and personal advancement, and may be somewhat modest, unassertive, and not very strategic about her career. As a manager, she will tend to be quiet, careful about following procedures, and won't often disagree with her superiors.

Recognition

Recognition motives are associated with a desire to be known, recognized, visible, even famous, and with a lifestyle guided by opportunities for self-display and dreams of achievement - whether or not they are actualized. Persons with high scores on this scale care deeply about being the center of attention and having their accomplishments acknowledged in public. They tend to be interesting, imaginative, self-confident, and dramatic, but also independent and unpredictable. High scores on Recognition seem especially important for successful careers in sales or politics. People with low scores on this scale tend to be described as modest, conforming, and generous.

If a person receives a *high* score on the Recognition scale, this suggests he is colorful, socially self-confident and impulsive, and handles pressure and criticism well. As a manager, he will prefer to work in teams, communicate very well with his staff, have lots of ideas, but he may have trouble admitting his mistakes. People with high scores on this scale tend to be described as dramatic, unusual, and reluctant to share credit.

If a person receives an *average* score on the Recognition scale, this suggests that, although he wants to be recognized for his achievements, he is also willing to share credit with others. Although public recognition is not the primary motivator in his life, he is not likely to remain silent when he is due some credit for important accomplishments.

If a person receives a *low* score on the Recognition scale, this suggests he tends to be modest and reserved and avoids calling attention to himself. As a manager, he will be quiet, perhaps somewhat uncommunicative, but willing to share credit with others, including subordinates.

Scientific

Scientific motives are associated with an interest in new ideas, new technology, an analytical approach to problem solving, and a lifestyle organized around learning, exploring, and understanding how things work. Persons with high scores on this scale care deeply about truth and getting below the surface noise to solve problems correctly. They tend to be bright, curious, and comfortable with technology, and choose careers in science, technology, medicine, higher education, and engineering. People with low scores on this scale tend to be described as responsive, flexible, and willing to admit mistakes.

If a person receives a *high* score on the Scientific scale, this suggests she is intellectually motivated, analytical, curious, inquiring, and she likes working with new technology. As a manager, she will tend to be on top of new technical and business information, well-organized and stable, and a hard-nosed and objective problem solver. People with high scores on this scale are also likely to be described as impatient, argumentative, and easily annoyed.

If a person receives an *average* score on the Scientific scale, this suggests that although she can analyze problems in a logical and rigorous way, she is also comfortable with intuitive ways of thinking. She is as likely to engage others in problem solving as she is to research ideas on her own.

If a person receives a *low* score on the Scientific scale, this suggests she is uninterested in science and technology, and she is more of an intuitive than an analytical problem solver. As a manager, she should be sympathetic, open to feedback, responsive to criticism, and more comfortable working with people than with technology.

Security

Security motives are associated with a need for structure, order, predictability, and a lifestyle organized around planning for the future and minimizing financial risk, employment uncertainty, and criticism. Persons with high scores on this scale care deeply about safety, financial security, and avoiding mistakes. They tend to be quiet, conforming, and cautious, but also punctual and easy to supervise. Such people tend to earn less than they might because they are unwilling to take risks with their careers. People with low scores tend to be described as independent, open to criticism, and willing to take risks.

If a person receives a *high* score on the Security scale, this suggests he is cautious, polite, and attentive to details, but somewhat shy and uncomfortable around strangers. As a manager he will tend to avoid risks and to be unassertive and reluctant to solicit feedback from his staff. People with high scores tend to be described as inhibited, conforming, and lacking leadership skills, and they need a sense of job security.

If a person receives an *average* score on the Security scale, this suggests he enjoys taking risks when appropriate but he would also rather be safe than sorry. He is not likely to perform well in situations where the chances of success are uncertain or where the future of the organization is in doubt.

If a person receives a *low* score on the Security scale, this suggests he is outgoing, leaderlike, and enjoys testing the limits. As a manager, he should be unafraid of taking risks, assertive, open to feedback from his staff, and unconcerned about job security.

Tradition

Traditional motives are associated with a concern for morality, high standards, family values, appropriate social behavior, and a lifestyle guided by well-established principles of conduct. Persons with high scores on this scale care about maintaining tradition, custom, and socially acceptable behavior. They tend to be trusting, considerate, responsive to advice, and comfortable in conservative organizations, but also set in their ways. Persons with low scores tend to be described as unconventional, progressive, and unpredictable.

If a person receives a *high* score on the Tradition scale, this suggests she is stable, conscientious, and good-natured, but somewhat cautious. As a manager, she will tend to be principled and even handed, but she may be somewhat resistant to change. People with high scores are also likely to be described as commonsensical, stable, and conservative.

If a person receives an *average* score on the Tradition scale, this suggests that, although she enjoys doing things in new ways, she also appreciates tradition and history as guides to behavior. She tends to appreciate both sides of political issues.

If a person receives a *low* score on the Tradition scale, this suggests she enjoys novelty, experimentation, and innovation, and she is somewhat liberal in her views. As a manager, she will tend to be flexible, impulsive, independent, unconventional, and willing to take risks.

Sample MVPI Profile Interpretations for Holland's Occupational Types

Holland's (1985a) model of vocational types is an exhaustive taxonomy for classifying personality characteristics required in occupations. Holland's model can categorize virtually every job in the Occupational Information Network (O*NET). This model provides a systematic method for thinking about the types of people found in organizations.

A Realistic Profile

In Holland's theory, Realistic types are practical, concrete, action oriented, and traditionally masculine - think of a soldier, a football coach, or a mechanical engineer. They are down-to-earth, technically oriented, compliant, and a bit introverted. Figure 4.1 is the profile of a firefighter who was the top student in a class of 100 at the fire academy in a medium sized southwestern city. Although the scale scores are clearly differentiated, the pattern shows some elevation across a number of scales, indicating a range of motives and interests. Mr. R received his highest scores for Scientific, Tradition, and Affiliation motives; he received his lowest scores for Aesthetic and Commercial. This suggests that he will be interested in how things work and their technical details (Scientific), he will seek work environments with standard operating procedures (Tradition), and value working with others (Affiliation). He will not be interested in art, music, literature, or attractive surroundings (Aesthetic) nor will he particularly be interested in business-related and financial matters (Commercial).

Figure 4.1

The MVPI Realistic Profile

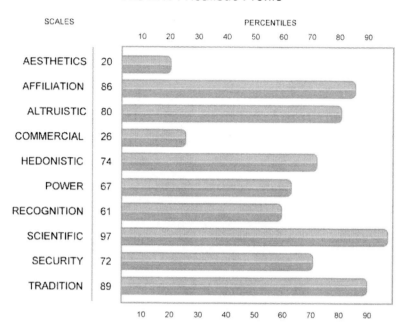

SCALES		PERCENTILES
AESTHETICS	20	
AFFILIATION	86	
ALTRUISTIC	80	
COMMERCIAL	26	
HEDONISTIC	74	
POWER	67	
RECOGNITION	61	
SCIENTIFIC	97	
SECURITY	72	
TRADITION	89	

Mr. R will be seen by his boss as conscientious, having good judgment, able to solve problems, working well with others, and being a good company man. Mr. R will be seen by his peers as willing to share credit for accomplishments, being a good team player, and staying on top of technical developments.

Mr. R's boss can best motivate him with opportunities to learn new skills and techniques. In particular, many fire departments offer in-service training that is very popular with professional firefighters, because of their interest in staying up to date on technology. Mr. R will not be motivated by salary bonuses or a chance to move into management with pay greater than that of a firefighter. This firefighter will work best in an environment that maintains conservative values (Tradition) and a job that allows him to take advantage of his analytical abilities (Scientific). He will most like to associate with people who share his conservative values, but who are friendly, helpful, analytical, and who like to get things done; conversely, he will avoid artists, liberals, and people who are preoccupied with their investments.

An Investigative Profile

In Holland's model, Investigative types are academics, researchers, people who are interested in ideas, principles, and abstractions. They tend to be somewhat introverted, rebellious, and, hopefully, creative. Figure 4.2 is the profile of a mid-career physician who is in line to be vice president and medical director of one of the largest petroleum companies in the United States. He completed the MVPI as part of an individualized assessment for career counseling. Dr. I claimed that, on the one hand, politics were preventing him from progressing in his current position and, on the other hand, he was reluctant to make waves or look for another medical director position.

Figure 4.2

The MVPI Investigative Profile

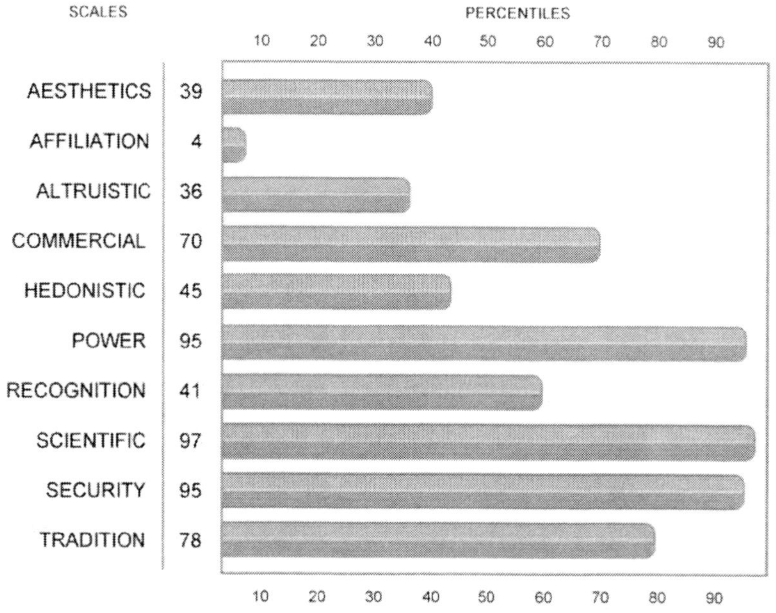

SCALES		PERCENTILES
AESTHETICS	39	
AFFILIATION	4	
ALTRUISTIC	36	
COMMERCIAL	70	
HEDONISTIC	45	
POWER	95	
RECOGNITION	41	
SCIENTIFIC	97	
SECURITY	95	
TRADITION	78	

Dr. I received his highest scores for Scientific, Power, and Security motives. He received his lowest scores for Affiliation, Altruistic, and Aesthetic motives. This suggests that he is interested in knowledge, research, and advanced technologies (Scientific) as well as control, success, and accomplishment (Power). In addition, he is careful, conservative, and uncomfortable with testing the limits (Security). He will not be interested in working closely with other people - which is probably the reason he avoids patients (Affiliation) - and he is not particularly sympathetic to the plight of the downtrodden (Altruistic) or concerned about staff morale.

Dr. I will be seen by his boss as having good judgment, being predictable, quiet, socially appropriate, and a good company citizen. Dr. I will be seen by his staff as having a vision for the department (Power), accepting challenges (Scientific), and a good organizational citizen (Security). However, they will also see him as avoiding close relationships (Affiliation), competitive (Power), and lacking a sense of humor (Security).

Dr. I's boss can best motivate him by giving him opportunities for intellectual growth and greater responsibility with the promise that these efforts will enhance his future. If his boss had a vision for the future, he would promise Dr. I a role in the succession plan upon the boss's retirement. Although Dr. I needs a position in which he can contribute and make a difference, he also needs job security. Dr. I is not particularly responsive to attention, approval, or praise - he doesn't want to be the center of attention - although he is not indifferent to money. He will work best in a corporate culture that emphasizes security and a dedication to old fashioned values. The people with whom he will most like to associate will be other ambitious, status seeking types; conversely, he will avoid artists, entertainers, and dilettantes.

An Artistic Profile

According to Holland's theory, Artistic types - writers, architects, poets, painters - are unconventional, somewhat troubled, and more interested in self-expression than money, power, and social acceptance. Figure 4.3 is an example of a competent, non-neurotic Artistic type. Ms. A is a successful interior designer in a large mid-western United States city. She is among the senior designers in a small firm specializing in residential properties. She is recognized locally for her work and, from time to time, has received awards for her designs. Ms. A received her highest scores for Aesthetic, Scientific, and Affiliation motives; she received her lowest scores for Tradition, Security, and Commercial motives.

This suggests that she will be interested in artistic activities and will enjoy creative self-expression (Aesthetic). In addition, she is also interested in creative problem solving (Scientific), especially when it requires working with others to generate solutions (Affiliation). She is not interested in conventional rituals (Tradition), or projects that require following procedures and "painting by the numbers" (Security).

Ms. A will be seen by her boss as easily bored, testing the limits, nonconforming, but interested in success. Ms. A will be seen by her coworkers as flexible, curious, a source of ideas, fun to be around, and flighty. Customers will like working with her.

Figure 4.3

The MVPI Artistic Profile

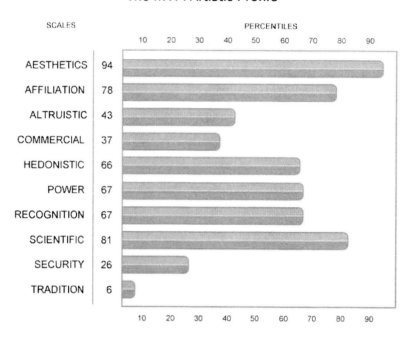

Ms. A's boss can best motivate her through opportunities to solve difficult design problems (Scientific) using her independent creative resources (Aesthetic) for people who appreciate her talents (Recognition). She will not be motivated by money or the assurance of enough projects to cover the employment needs of her immediate future. She will work best in a corporate climate that allows her to exercise her imagination through designs where product appearance is a central value. The people with whom she will most like to associate are other creative types who also like people and environments that are pleasurable and fun. She will avoid preachers, conservative politicians, and bureaucrats.

A Social Profile

Figure 4.4 is the profile of Holland's Social type. Social occupations involve helping others and providing service; social types tend to be altruistic, idealistic, unconventional, and somewhat self-sacrificing (e.g., Mother Teresa). Very successful Social types may often be better classified as Enterprising types (see discussion below), because they have a greater desire for power and influence than for social justice and helping the needy.

Figure 4.4

The MVPI Social Profile

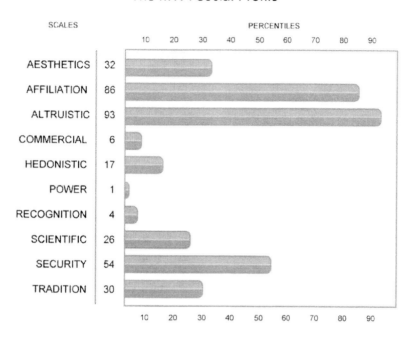

Mrs. S began her career as a registered nurse. She was an only child who sought opportunities to be with and to help other people. She nursed seriously ill research subjects. While raising her children, she volunteered for the community service charities Meals-on-Wheels and the American Red Cross. She recently returned to nursing on the staff of the Red Cross. As seen in Figure 4.4, Mrs. S has a very well differentiated profile. She received her highest scores for Altruistic and Affiliation; she received her lowest scores for Power, Recognition, and Commercial. This suggests that she is primarily interested in caring for people's needs (Altruistic) and she enjoys social interaction (Affiliation). She is clearly not interested in money (Commercial), authority (Power), or attention from others (Recognition).

Mrs. S will be seen by her boss as sympathetic and trusting (Altruistic) as well as working well with new people and willing to confide in others (Affiliation). Mrs. S will be seen by her coworkers as calm under pressure and willing to give feedback that makes others feel good (Altruistic). In addition, she will spend time getting others to work together and to keep them informed (Affiliation).

Mrs. S's boss can best motivate her by providing opportunities to make other people feel good and contribute to their development. She will not be motivated by money, awards, citations, or opportunities to assume leadership roles. She will work best in a corporate climate where the welfare of others is the shared mission. The people with whom she will most like to associate are altruistic types who dedicate themselves to improving the lives of others. She will avoid accountants, regulators, politicians, and mean-spirited gossipers.

An Enterprising Profile

Enterprising people, according to Holland, are ambitious, upwardly mobile, socially skilled, and somewhat conforming. They are achievement oriented, and they enjoy being in charge of others. The MVPI profile in Figure 4.5 is an example of the enterprising type. Mr. E is a senior vice president and odds-on-favorite for CEO at one of the largest transportation companies in the United States. He has a well differentiated pattern of motives. He received his highest scores for Commercial, Power, Scientific, and Tradition motives; he received his lowest scores for Affiliation, Altruistic, and Hedonistic. This suggests that he will enjoy getting things done (Power), working on financial (Commercial) problems (Scientific), and maintaining established customs and high standards (Tradition). He will not be interested in working with others (Affiliation), charitable activities (Altruistic), or partying (Hedonistic).

Figure 4.5

The MVPI Enterprising Profile

SCALES		PERCENTILES
AESTHETICS	32	
AFFILIATION	21	
ALTRUISTIC	27	
COMMERCIAL	81	
HEDONISTIC	4	
POWER	83	
RECOGNITION	47	
SCIENTIFIC	76	
SECURITY	32	
TRADITION	78	

Mr. E will be seen by his boss as having leadership skills, being assertive and testing the limits, being stable and conscientious, and being a strategic problem solver. Mr. E will be seen by his subordinates as being hard working, an innovator, impatient and inconsiderate when the work load is heavy and serious (and probably not a lot of fun).

Mr. E's boss can best motivate him by providing opportunities to solve difficult problems that have financial implications. In fact, Mr. E was consumed by a project he invented to restructure the entire pricing system for transportation services. Mr. E will not be motivated by opportunities to accrue more vacation time. He will work best in a corporate culture that emphasizes productivity and

Interpretations & Uses

accomplishment (Power) and attainment of financial goals (Commercial). The people he will most like to associate with will be other high status, ambitious people, financial analysts, and entrepreneurs; conversely, he will avoid artists, social workers, and anyone who doesn't seem serious about his or her career.

A Conventional Profile

Conventional people, according to Holland, are in many ways the psychological opposite of Artistic types. They are careful, conforming, attentive to detail, and willing to follow instructions. Figure 4.6 is a good example of a Conventional type. Mr. C is an accountant by training who has developed a small real estate investment firm. Although he heads the firm, he spends most of his time maintaining the records and monitoring the finances of the business; it is his partners who locate the business opportunities and find the investors. In his spare time, Mr. C is very involved in the Baptist church and is an active participant on several committees.

He received his highest scores for Tradition, Commercial, and Power motives. He received his lowest scores for Affiliation, Altruistic, Recognition, and Security motives. This suggests that Mr. C is interested in conservative politics (Tradition), financial matters and opportunities to save or make money (Commercial), and he values achievement and advancement (Power). Conversely, Mr. C is not particularly interested in social interaction and will not seek opportunities to meet new people (Affiliation), nor is he interested in traditional liberal causes such as helping the downtrodden or fighting human rights abuses (Altruistic). Mr. C's church activities probably do not extend to feeding the homeless.

Figure 4.6

The MVPI Conventional Profile

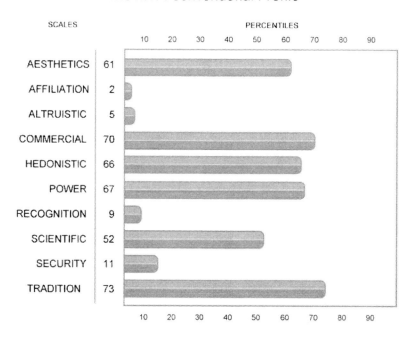

SCALES		PERCENTILES
AESTHETICS	61	
AFFILIATION	2	
ALTRUISTIC	5	
COMMERCIAL	70	
HEDONISTIC	66	
POWER	67	
RECOGNITION	9	
SCIENTIFIC	52	
SECURITY	11	
TRADITION	73	

Mr. C will be seen by his board as serious, tough-minded, predictable, hard working, responsible, and having good judgment. Mr. C. will be seen by his subordinates as impatient, disagreeable with clients, noncommunicative, and unconcerned with helping others learn new skills. Although subordinates may describe Mr. C as having a vision for the company, they will also say that they are not proud to be part of his team.

Mr. C's board can best motivate him by providing opportunities for him to continue expanding the business, where the expansion is deliberate, conservative, and well-planned. He will also be motivated by financial rewards and successes. He will not be concerned about staff morale. In addition, he seems not to require recognition for his accomplishments, which is probably why he is not particularly sensitive to signs of disrespect from others. Mr. C will perform best in a climate that allows him to work hard, analyze financial problems, and make money. The people with whom he will most like to associate are conservative political players with some status. He will not enjoy interacting with social workers, human resource specialists, psychologists, and environmentalists.

Uses

There are three primary uses for the MVPI. The first use for the MVPI is in selection contexts, examining the degree of person-job or person-organization fit. The relative fit can be determined by comparing a person's higher scores on the MVPI with the prevailing values of the organization. Research by Holland, Schneider, and others shows that people are happiest working in environments that are compatible or consistent with their core values. So, for example, a person with strong Altruistic motives will tend to be uncomfortable working in a financial services company where the orientation is toward profit rather than staff morale. Similarly, a person with strong Security needs would be uncomfortable working in a company like a securities trading firm where taking risks is part of the business.

Within a development context, there are two applicable uses of the MVPI. The MVPI can be used as a tool for career planning. Each scale on the inventory contains a subscale for vocational choice. Thus persons with high scores for Aesthetic motives should choose a career that includes opportunities for creative self-expression. Persons with high scores for Altruistic motives should choose a career that provides opportunities to help others. The Hedonistic, Power, Security, and Tradition scales don't lead to clear vocational recommendations; rather they concern people's needs for fun, achievement, security, and liberal versus conservative values. The other scales make straight forward career recommendations.

Additionally, the inventory can be used for staff development and feedback. Understanding employees' values can help managers to better motivate their subordinates. People with low scores on the Commercial scale are not interested in or motivated by money. A smart manager will find some other way to motivate these people. Similarly, a person with strong Power needs will be motivated by opportunities to get things done and make a mark on an organization whereas persons with weak Power needs are indifferent to such considerations. Within groups, MVPI results can be used to help team members better understand areas of conflict and help organizations quantify their unique culture. Further, a manager's MVPI profile will determine the working environment they create for their employees. Understanding the overlap between subordinate and manager profiles may help to decrease conflict and create a more understanding work environment.

CHAPTER 5

ADMINISTERING THE MVPI

As a publisher of psychological assessments, Hogan provides a state-of-the-art administration platform developed to meet the needs of clients. Since the mid 1990's, the delivery for the MVPI has been through a web-based assessment platform. The assessment platform was designed and is maintained for security, ease of use, speed, and flexibility. The platform uses leading edge technologies such as web services, middleware, and XML. The flexibility of these technologies allows customized solutions appropriate for clients of all sizes. An overview of key features of this system is presented below. For further information please contact Hogan's Customer Service Department at 1-800-756-0632 or customerservice@hoganassessments.com. Office hours are 8am-5pm (U.S. Central Time) and after hours messages are checked daily.

Key Features of the Web-Based Platform

It is important for test administrators to understand how participants complete an online assessment, be able to address questions or concerns participants may raise, and use test administrator tools. To address these issues, Hogan trains administrators in the functionality of the Hogan system. In the initial training session, an administrator is instructed on how to create participant ID's as well as how to use various other tools on the administrative website. Additional training is available for the creation of participant groups, obtaining reports, changing report options, and specifying report delivery options.

Hogan's testing system is fully redundant, using a multi-location systems architecture ensuring its constant availability. Clients can access the testing platform 24 hours a day, 7 days a week, from any Internet-enabled computer. Test results are normally delivered in 90 seconds or less, making results nearly instantaneous. Results are provided to the client via the web or through e-mail as an attached encrypted PDF file. Hogan consults with outside security experts to ensure data security; using 128 bit secure access via password protection when safe guarding clients' and user assessment data.

All Hogan web ordering systems allow Hogan to tailor the ordering and reporting experience to each user based on a hierarchical system of client and user preferences. Users can select from a wide variety of MVPI report options including: simple graphic reports, data reports, individual reports, group-level reports, and specialty reports.

Whether a client orders from a single office or numerous locations, all orders can flow through a single account. Hogan product-level security features allow clients to restrict individual user's ability to order and view reports on a product-by-product basis.

Completing the MVPI Using the Online System

This section provides an example of the participant experience when completing the MVPI online. Testing time for the MVPI requires approximately twenty minutes, but may vary depending on the test taker's reading speed.

Once a participant receives a User ID from the administrator, he/she logs into the specified website, such as http://www.gotohogan.com or a customized portal designed for Hogan clients. To log on to the website, a minimum version of Microsoft Internet Explorer 4.0 or Netscape Navigator 6.2 is needed. Once at the website, the individual sees a login page similar to the one in Figure 5.1.

Figure 5.1

Hogan Assessment Systems Participant Login Web Page

At the login page, the participant is asked to enter his/her assigned User ID and password (e.g., User ID: BB123456; Password = SAMPLE) and then select the Logon button. The participant is prompted to fill out a brief demographics page (see Figure 5.2) and agree to an informed consent clause (see section 5.3). This clause outlines information regarding the purpose, administration, and results of the assessments.

On the Participant Information web page, the participant can insert a string of numbers when asked to input his/her Employee ID or SSN. An administrator may choose to have the individual enter his/her actual social security number, but for privacy reasons we suggest using an ID designed for internal tracking purposes, such as an Employee ID number. Once the user has logged into the system, he/she will be asked to create a personal password and complete additional demographic information. When all of the required fields are complete, the participant must select Submit to continue.

Figure 5.2

Hogan Assessment Systems Participant Information Web Page

After clicking the Submit button, the user is redirected to the Participant Menu. The Participant Menu displays each assessment they are assigned to take (see figure 5.3). If the individual is taking multiple assessments, each will be listed. After an assessment is completed, the individual is returned to this menu to select and proceed with additional assessments until all assigned inventories are completed.

Figure 5.3

Hogan Assessment Systems Participant Menu Web Page

It is important that the administrator emphasize the need to respond to every question. If the respondent leaves more than 1/3 of items blank, the report will be invalid. The participant should not spend too much time on any one specific statement; there are no "right" or "wrong" answers. The participant can navigate forward and backward through the assessment. He/she may select the Next button to continue the assessment; the Previous button permits viewing the previous page. Because the assessment does not time out, the participant can stop and start the assessment at will. If at any time the individual discontinues the assessment, all prior submitted information will be retained. The participant can log back into the system with his/her User ID and self-created personal password to continue at any time. Once completed, the participant submits the assessment. Results are processed through a scoring engine that generates and sends the report to an e-mail address(es) designated by the administrator. A sample of an Assessment Questionnaire web page is presented in Figure 5.4.

If the account administrator or the participant experiences a problem, they are encouraged to contact Hogan's Customer Service Department at 1-800-756-0632 or customerservice@hoganassessments.com.

Figure 5.4

Hogan Assessment Systems Questionnaire Assessment Web Page

Participant's Informed Consent

Hogan operates under the assumption that all individuals who take assessments have given their informed consent to participate in the assessment process. This is the fundamental concept that underlies all current and anticipated data protection protocols and legislation.

In order for individuals taking the assessments to give their informed consent, they must understand the purpose of the assessment, the likely use of the assessment data, and how the data are protected. These protocols are described below and are binding on all Hogan clients and individuals taking the assessments. Failure to comply with any of these safeguards will constitute grounds for termination of any data transfer arrangements between Hogan and the person(s) or entity(ies) concerned. The Candidate Log-on Entry protocol requires all individuals taking the assessment to give their informed consent before they can complete the assessment process.

Purpose

The assessments on the website were created to provide personal characteristic information and feedback to trained and accredited consultants and HR professionals. These data are primarily used for selection and/or development.

Data Use and Storage

The assessment data will only be used by trained and accredited consultants or HR professionals. Hogan will retain individual raw data for a period of three years and, in addition, will use anonymously held (identifying information removed) aggregated data for normative studies. All Hogan clients are responsible for complying with national and international protocols covering data use and storage.

Access to Data

Hogan will not provide results directly to individuals taking the assessments. The dissemination of results is the sole responsibility of the requesting organization. Individuals taking the assessments are not guaranteed access to their individual results.

Primary Security

In order to safeguard individual results, the website contains only the assessment items, not the assessment programs (which are held by Hogan and its clients). It is impossible to process results through the website. Results can only be processed by downloading the raw data, decrypting the raw data, and scoring these data with appropriate programs. Until that time, responses to assessment items are merely encrypted alphanumeric strings with no discernible meaning.

Individuals taking the assessments are provided a username and password to access the website assessments. In addition, the raw data are encrypted. Each organization using the web site is provided with a secure method of data transfer from the Internet to their organization.

Using International Translations of the MVPI

As the test publisher, Hogan undertakes translation and localization initiatives to brand and make available its assessment tools internationally. As of the publication of this manual, MVPI translations can be accessed in thirty-seven languages. Additional translations are completed as needed. A list of current language availability appears in Table 5.1.

Table 5.1

MVPI Language Translations/Adaptations Available Online

Arabic	Korean (KO)
Australian (AU)	Macedonian (MA)
Bahasa Indonesian (BI)	New Zealand English
Bahasa Malaysian (BM)	Norwegian (NO)
Brazilian Portuguese (BP)	Polish (PL)
Bulgarian (BG)	Romanian (RO)
Castilian Spanish (CA)	Russian (RU)
Czech (CS)	Serbia
Danish (DA)	Simplified Chinese (ZH)
French Canadian (FC)	Slovak (SK)
French Parisian (FR)	South African (AE)
German (GR)	Spanish (ES)
Greek (EL)	Swedish (SV)
Greek English (GE)	Thai (TH)
Icelandic (IS)	Traditional Chinese (ZC)
Indian (IN)	Turkish (TR)
Italian (IT)	UK English (UK)
Japanese (JA)	US English (US)
Kenya (KE)	

Translations of the MVPI are administered through the Hogan web based assessment platform. The administrator can choose to assess participants in multiple languages and also choose to produce MVPI reports in various languages. MVPI report translations are selected when the User ID is generated from the online system, as illustrated in Figure 5.5

Figure 5.5

Hogan Assessment Systems Report Language Selection

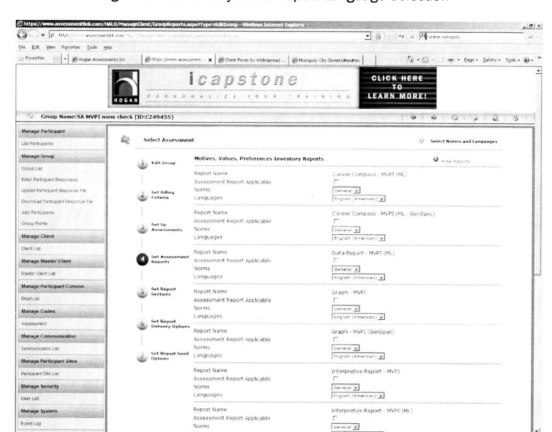

After creating a participant's online User ID for the desired report language, the administrator directs the participant to the Hogan multi-language assessment website. To log on to the website, a minimum version of Microsoft Internet Explorer 4.0 or Netscape Navigator 6.2 is needed. Once the participant logs on to the website, he/she may choose to take the MVPI in any of the languages represented by the country flags illustrated in Figure 5.6 by selecting the flag. Then, the login page will appear in the chosen language and the participant is asked to enter his/her assigned User ID and password (e.g., User ID BB123456, Password = SAMPLE) and select the Login button. The participant is prompted to fill out a brief demographics page and agree to an informed consent clause (see Section 5.3).

Figure 5.6

Hogan Assessment Systems Language Translation Flags

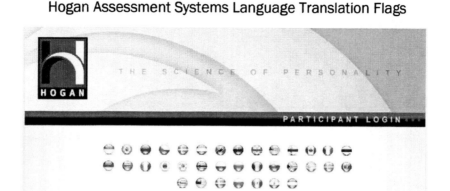

On the Participant Information web page, the participant can insert any string of numbers when asked to input his/her SSN or Employee ID number. Some countries do not use a SSN or have legislation prohibiting the collection of this information. In these cases, the participant should be told what to input into this field by his/her administrator. An administrator may select to have the participant enter his/her employee ID, User ID, or a company assigned ID designed for internal tracking purposes. The system requests that the participant create a personal password. This becomes the participant's new password for logging out and back into the system. Once all fields on the Participant Information page are complete, the participant selects Submit to continue (see Figure 5.7).

Figure 5.7

Hogan Assessment Systems Participant Information Page

After completing the Participant Information page, the participant is ready to start the assessment. Figure 5.8 shows the Participant Menu web page. If the participant is set up to take multiple assessments, each will be listed in the Participant Menu. The participant selects the assessment from the Participant Menu and the assessment is delivered in the desired language chosen earlier from the Hogan Multi-Language test administration website (e.g., Figure 5.9).

Figure 5.8

Hogan Assessment Systems Participant Menu

Figure 5.9

Hogan Assessment Systems Multilanguage Questionnaire Example Web Page

Accommodating Individuals with Disabilities

The Americans with Disabilities Act of 1990 (ADA) is the most significant, recent employment law that addresses employers' requirements for fair treatment of disabled individuals. It prohibits discrimination against qualified individuals with disabilities in employment. This law has important implications for employers' procedures used in interviewing, testing, and hiring new employees. For pre-employment testing, the ADA specifies that employers must provide alternate forms of employment testing that "accurately (assess) the skills, aptitudes, or whatever other factor of such applicant or employee that such test purports to measure, rather than reflecting the impaired sensory, manual or speaking skills of such employee or applicant" Sec. 102(b)(7), 42 U.S.C.A.Sec. 12112. Hogan complies with the ADA requirements by working with clients to accommodate individuals with special needs. Large print assessments and screen readers are available from customer service at 1-800-756-0632 or customerservice@hoganassessments.com. In addition, because the MVPI is not a timed test, individuals can take as much time as they need to complete the assessment. Hogan can make additional accommodations on a case by case basis through contacting customer service.

Frequently Asked Questions

The following are questions participants ask frequently, followed by answers typically given by customer service staff:

Q. I am trying to sign back in to complete the assessments but my User ID and password are not working.

A. Please use the new personal password you created when you first accessed the system. (You were requested to change the password on the initial participant information screen).

Q. Can I stop the assessment at any time?

A. Yes, you can select the Stop Assessment link to end your session. Please make note of your User ID and new personal password in order to log back into the website.

Q. How long will the assessments take?

A. Please allow 15 to 20 minutes to complete the assessment.

Q. Is it a timed assessment?

A. No. You can take as much time as needed to complete the inventory.

Q. Will I receive a copy of my results?

A. We are not at liberty to share or discuss results with candidates. Results are sent to the company that requested your assessments; the company decides whether or not to share results with you.

Q. My system locked up before I completed the assessment – were all my responses lost?

A. No. Your responses are saved after each page is completed.

CHAPTER 6

COMPILATION OF NORMS

Importance of Norms for Interpretation and Decision-Making

Raw assessment scores hold very little information without appropriate norms to provide context for their interpretation. According to Nunnally (1967, p. 244), "norms are any scores that provide a frame of reference for interpreting the scores of particular persons." As such, norms are vital for providing meaningful context for interpreting assessment scores and subsequent decision-making. However, it is the *quality* of those norms that is of particular importance. By using accurate and up-to-date norms, users can examine one person's scores against a suitable comparison group and, relative to those others, draw conclusions about that person's predicted future behavior.

Presentation of Normative Data

Assessment providers use a variety of formats to present normative data. However, three formats are most prevalent: (a) raw scale scores, (b) standardized scores, or (c) percentile ranks (Nunnally, 1967). Although raw scale scores directly link to the assessment, they are difficult to interpret because different assessments and scales have differing total possible scores. For example, a raw scale score of "8" is difficult to interpret because the total possible score could be 10, 50, 100, 1000, or any other score. Depending on the total possible score, one would interpret a raw scale score of "8" in vastly different lights.

To address the problems with interpreting raw scale scores, some assessment publishers provide norms in the form of standardized scores. Standardized scores are expressed using a mean and a standard deviation, although these vary depending on the type of standardized score used. For example, *z-scores* use a mean of 0 and standard deviation of 1. Alternatively, *T-scores* use a mean of 50 and standard deviation of 10. *Sten scores* use a mean of 5.5 and standard deviation of 2. As these examples illustrate, standardized scores transform an individual's raw scale score into a ranking metric, but these score ranges vary and, like raw scores, are not easily understood.

Unlike the two methods previously described, we specify that the MVPI be interpreted using percentile ranks. Percentile ranks represent an alternative to standardized scores. Like standardized scores, percentiles place an individual's raw scale score on a ranking metric where users can compare one person's scores against others' scores. However, unlike standardized scores with ranges of -3 to +3 (z-scores), 20 to 80 (T-scores), or 1 to 10 (Sten scores), percentile ranks use a 0 – 100% range, most commonly understood and easily interpreted by the general public. For example, a raw Affiliation scale score may correspond to a z-score of 1.1. However, it is difficult to interpret this standardized score. That same scale score may correspond to a percentile score of 85%, facilitating the easy interpretation that this person scores above 85% of others on that scale.

Professional Standards for Norm Development

Cronbach (1984) noted that the norms for many psychological assessments are "notoriously inadequate" and emphasized the importance of using appropriate samples when calculating norms. To provide norms, assessment providers collect data from "suitable and representative" individuals in the assessment's intended population(s). Specifically, Cronbach provided four standards for developing adequate norms, stating that they should: (a) consist of individuals for whom the assessment was intended and against whom examinees will be compared, (b) represent the referent population, (c) include a sufficient number of cases, and (d) be appropriately subdivided. Also, practical and professional considerations encourage assessment providers to establish and maintain norms. For example, Standard 4.6 of the *Standards for Educational and Psychological Testing* (AERA, APA, & NCME, 1999) states:

> *Reports of norming studies should include precise specification of the population that was sampled, sampling procedures and participation rates, any weighting of the sample, the dates of testing, and descriptive statistics. The information provided should be sufficient to enable users to judge the appropriateness of the norms for interpreting the scores of local examinees. Technical documentation should indicate the precision of the norms themselves. (p. 55)*

Hogan developed and presents normative data for the MVPI using an extensive normative sample based on the intended use of the assessment among the Hogan client base. We divided these norms by occupational and demographic variables of interest. Using percentile ranks, these normative data are easily interpretable, facilitating decision-making in applied personnel contexts. As discussed in subsequent sections of this chapter, these considerations ensure that MVPI norms adhere to existing professional guidelines and standards. The remainder of this chapter describes the process of developing normative data for the MVPI, satisfying the requirement previously outlined by the *Standards for Educational and Psychological Testing* (AERA, APA, & NCME, 1999).

Updating Norms for the 2010 MVPI

Hogan uses the MVPI as a developmental assessment for providing working adults with information about their motives, values, and interests. After empirical validation, Hogan also uses the MVPI as a selection assessment to evaluate fit between an individual's values and organizational culture. Across these applications, the target population of the MVPI remains the same – "working adults." This population includes those in positions of authority (i.e., managers and executives), expert employees with responsibilities to others (i.e., professionals), those interacting frequently with customers or clients (i.e., sales and customer support), and those providing administrative services (i.e., administrative and clerical). Although the MVPI is used for a variety of jobs, these four groups provide the core development and selection applications of the assessment. Therefore, these four groups represent the primary samples we used to establish and maintain normative data for interpretation and decision-making.

It is common for authors and publishers to invest considerable resources on norming during initial assessment development. However, it is less common to devote similar levels of organizational resources to *maintain and update* those norms after they are established. In our view, this is unfortunate because there is a professional responsibility to develop and maintain relevant norms.

Existing norms may require maintenance and/or updates for many reasons, but five key factors may significantly influence existing norms and signal a need for their evaluation, revision, and/or replacement:

1. Samples used to calculate existing norms may become outdated
2. New respondents may be more familiar with the assessment than previous respondents
3. Individuals and groups asked to contribute to normative samples may change
4. The purpose and/or application of the assessment may change
5. Representation of the norming samples may change with demographic/occupational shifts

Due to these and other changes, assessment providers should monitor, maintain, and update their norms when they observe the above-described conditions. Unfortunately, some assessments require renorming more often than others; no universal guidance is available on the frequency for updating norms. However, if normative data are to serve their intended purpose of providing an accurate context for score interpretation, assessment providers should occasionally recalibrate the frames of reference for their products. In fact, the 1999 *Standards for Educational and Psychological Testing* reiterates this point, stating in Standard 4.18:

> If a publisher provides norms for use in test score interpretation, then so long as the test remains in print, it is the publisher's responsibility to assure that the test is renormed with sufficient frequency to permit continued accurate and appropriate score interpretations. (p.59)

Due to this professional responsibility, Hogan investigated the score distributions for all MVPI scales in early 2009. Relative to Joyce and Robert Hogan's first publication of the MVPI norms in 1996, we noted in this research that the score distributions for all MVPI scales changed slightly. Consequently, the value of prior normative data for selection and development applications is restricted. For example, in a selection context, selection cutoff scores based on prior norms would no longer result in the same balanced pass rates observed in earlier years. Likewise, in the context of personnel development, using prior norms might slightly distort interpretive information such as feedback because a raw scale score may not be associated with the same normative percentile rank previously recorded. For these reasons, Hogan decided to update the MVPI norms to ensure the accuracy and timeliness of the data providing a basis for interpretation and subsequent decision-making.

To develop a comprehensive sampling strategy for updating the MVPI norms, we identified stratification variables. These variables served as criteria to ensure that the new MVPI norms achieve proportionate representation of respondents across these groups. We identified five key stratification variables that guided the development of the new 2010 MVPI norms. We describe each of these concepts in further detail below:

1. Job Families
2. Application of Data
3. Race/Ethnicity
4. Sex
5. Age

Job Families

Job families represent clusters of occupations grouped together based on the similarity of work performed, skills, education, training, and other credentials required for successful job performance. Hogan derived the seven job families, identified as the first stratification variable, from nine "job classifications" used by the Equal Employment Opportunity Commission (EEOC) for U.S. employers. Hogan uses this occupational system for two main reasons: (a) a large percentage of U.S. employers are familiar with the EEOC job classification system, and (b) the job classifications are conceptually clear and easy to use as a stratification variable.

Table 6.1 presents the seven Hogan job families, as well as the U.S. Department of Labor's (DoL) job categories included in each job family. The DoL developed these job categories in response to a growing need for an occupational classification system to classify all jobs within the U.S. workforce (U.S. Department of Labor, 1991). As such, Table 6.1 represents a crosswalk that Hogan clients and other users can reference to find the Hogan job family corresponding with many jobs in the United States economy.

Table 6.1

Hogan Job Family Structure with Department of Labor Job Categories

Hogan Job Family	Description	DoL Job Category
Managers & Executives	Employees assigned to positions of administrative or managerial authority over the human, physical, and financial resources of the organization.	Management Occupations
Professionals	Employees with little legitimate authority, but high status within the organization because of the knowledge and/or skills they possess. These employees are usually experts with a broad educational background, and rely primarily on their knowledge and intellect to perform their duties.	Architecture and Engineering Occupations Arts, Design, Entertainment, Sports, and Media Occupations Business and Financial Operations Occupations Community and Social Service Occupations Education, Training, and Library Occupations Health Practitioners and Technical Occupations Legal Occupations Life, Physical, and Social Science Occupations
Technicians & Specialists	Employees who rely on the application of highly specific knowledge in skilled manipulation (e.g., operation, repair, cleaning, and/or preparation) of specialized technology, tools, and/or machinery.	Installation, Maintenance, and Repair Occupations Computer and Mathematical Occupations
Operations & Trades	Craft workers (skilled), operatives (semi-skilled), and laborers (unskilled) whose job knowledge and skills are primarily gained through on-the-job training and experience; little pre-requisite knowledge or skill is needed.	Building and Grounds Cleaning and Maintenance Occupations Construction and Extraction Occupations Farming, Fishing, and Forestry Occupations Military Specific Production Occupations Transportation and Material Moving Occupations
Sales & Customer Support	Employees who use appropriate interpersonal style and communication techniques to establish relationships, sell products or services that fulfill customers' needs, and provide courteous and helpful service to customers after the sale.	Sales and Related Occupations
Administrative & Clerical	Employees who plan, direct, or coordinate supportive services of an organization. The main function of these employees is to facilitate the function of professionals by completing jobs that require little formal education or skills to complete (e.g., professional assistants, secretaries, clerks)	Healthcare Support Occupations Office and Administrative Support Occupations

Table 6.1 (Continued)

Hogan Job Family Structure with Department of Labor Job Categories

Hogan Job Family	Description	DoL Job Category
Service & Support	Employees that perform protective services for individuals and communities (e.g., police, firefighters, guards) and non-protective services for individuals that require little or no formal training but a high degree of interaction with people (e.g., food service, recreation and amusement).	Food Preparation and Serving Related Occupations Personal Care and Service Occupations Protective Service Occupations

As previously described, the primary target population of the MVPI includes four of the job families described above: (a) Managers and Executives, (b) Professionals, (c) Sales and Customer Support, and (d) Administrative and Clerical. Therefore, in developing the 2010 MVPI norms, Hogan sought to maximize representation of those four key job families. However, we also sought out data for the other three job families to ensure that the MVPI norms represented all jobs across the broad spectrum of the U.S. economy. These criteria guided the first level of data stratification during development of the 2010 MVPI norms.

Application of Data

Because the MVPI is used for both development and selection applications, Hogan balanced representation of the inventory data across these contexts. Specifically, we selected approximately the same number of selection and development cases and included only a small percentage of cases with unknown application. We also coded for job family when available and included cases representative of all seven job families, with an emphasis on the four representing the primary target population of the MVPI. The first two stratification levels ensure that the 2010 MVPI norms account for various applications of the data across the U.S. workforce and the target populations described previously.

Race/Ethnicity

To ensure that the updated MVPI norms represent respondents across racial/ethnic groups, we included race/ethnicity as a primary demographic stratification variable. We sought to identify cases of MVPI data available for respondents across multiple demographic categories. Consistent with forms used by the Equal Employment Opportunity Commission's (EEOC; 2006) Office of Management and Budget (OMB) to collect federal data on race and ethnicity in the workplace, we included five racial categories: (a) American Indian or Alaska Native, (b) Asian, (c) Black or African-American, (d) Native Hawaiian or Other Pacific Islander, and (e) White. In keeping with the EEOC guidelines, we included one ethnic category: (f) Hispanic or Latino, in this effort. However, in an environment where an increasing number of individuals include themselves with more than one racial or ethnic group, we also aimed to identify cases of MVPI data where respondents identified with (g) Two or More Races.

In sum, we sought to locate available MVPI cases representing the above seven racial and ethnic groups. We intended for the representation of these cases to approximate those found in the U.S. working population. To enhance the total number of cases in the normative dataset, we allowed for the inclusion of an appropriate number of cases with missing race/ethnicity data.

Sex

Sex represented our second demographic stratification variable. Similar to race/ethnicity, we used federal laws and guidelines from the EEOC to ensure proportionate representation of both sexes in the 2010 normative MVPI data. Specifically, we sought to identify cases of available MVPI data completed by males and females, and include proportionate numbers of male cases and female cases in the normative dataset. We intended to approximate the representation of men and women found in the U.S. working population, although to maintain adequate representation across other stratification variables, the final dataset contained a higher percentage of males. To enhance the total number of cases in the normative dataset, we allowed for the inclusion of an appropriate number of cases with missing sex data.

Age

Finally, we attempted to locate a representative sample of MVPI respondents across age groups. Consistent with the Age Discrimination in Employment Act of 1967 (ADEA; Lindemann & Grossman, 1996), our intent was to include proportionate numbers of data from respondents who were under 40 years of age when they completed the MVPI, as well as respondents 40 years of age or older. We sought to reflect the levels of these groups found in the U.S. working population. As with race/ethnicity and sex, we allowed for the inclusion of cases with missing age data to enhance the total number of cases in the normative dataset.

Our sampling strategy in compiling data to update the MVPI norms required the identification of cases that simultaneously satisfied the requirements of two occupational variables (i.e., job family, application of data) and three demographic variables (i.e., ethnicity, sex, age). By proportionately sampling representative cases from these groups, our sampling goals involved:

- Including cases across job families in the normative sample that represent the U.S. workforce, with emphasis on specific target populations of: (a) Managers and Executives, (b) Professionals, (c) Sales and Customer Support, and (d) Administrative and Clerical.

- Including an approximately equal representation of selection and development cases, with an emphasis on the four job families representing the MVPI's target population.

- Selecting cases to ensure demographic representation of seven total race/ethnicity groups, consistent with the EEOC (1978) guidelines: (a) American Indian or Alaska Native, (b) Asian, (c)

Black or African-American, (d) Native Hawaiian or Other Pacific Islander, (e) White, (f) Hispanic or Latino, and (g) Two or More Races. The proportionate representation of these groups is similar to levels found in the U.S. working population.

- Selecting cases to ensure adequate representation of both males and females.

- Selecting cases to ensure adequate representation of two age groups: (a) Under 40 Years, and (b) Age 40 and Over.

Driven by our professional responsibility to maintain accurate and current norms, and guided by our five key variables of interest along with the record keeping guidelines outlined by the EEOC (1978), we identified samples from the Hogan data warehouse. We next describe this sampling process.

Stratified Sampling of the Norming Population

Initial Population

Using the sampling plan described above, we drew representative samples from the Hogan data warehouse. We included data collected on-line between February 26, 2003 and February 2, 2008 in this initial population. We included cases from each of the Hogan job families previously described, with emphasis placed on Managers and Executives, Professionals, Sales and Customer Support, and Administrative and Clerical job families as a large preliminary "population" of the MVPI. Additionally, we included both selection and development cases.

Elimination of Cases

We then removed test cases from the dataset and cases with excessive missing data. For each 20-item scale in the MVPI, we define "excessive" missing data as at least two items on three of the five themes. At a minimum, a respondent must answer three or more items across three of the five themes for the scale to be valid for scoring. Consistent with this logic, we eliminated all cases where respondents failed to answer enough items to receive scores on each MVPI scale. Next, because Hogan has translated the MVPI into over 20 languages, and because no two translations can be considered perfectly equivalent, we regularly develop translation-specific norms. Therefore, for the current norm, we retained only English cases of the assessment. This resulted in a dataset containing MVPI results for 68,565 individuals.

After including sufficient cases to account for occupational stratification variables (i.e., Hogan job family, selection or development application of data), we obtained population estimates from the U.S. Census Bureau's American FactFinder (2006) program to specify general demographic characteristics for the normative database. Specifically, we used the latest population estimates available, collected in July 2006, to determine the current representation rates of various age, sex, and race/ethnicity groups in the U.S. population. We then compared the current demographic representation of our sample with the U.S. population. Results indicated that demographic representation of the normative sample was sufficiently similar to the demographic representation of the U.S. workforce. Therefore, we retained all 68,565 cases for the MVPI normative dataset.

Representativeness of the Norming Sample

The final normative sample by occupational designation appears in Table 6.2. To reflect the Hogan client base and balance demographic characteristics (i.e., age, sex, race/ethnicity), we included 25,321 cases with unknown occupational categories. Most of these represent development cases, where job information is frequently unavailable.

Table 6.2

Norming Sample Distribution by Hogan Job Family

Hogan Job Family	Number	Percent
Managers & Executives	22,252	32.5
Professionals	1,781	2.6
Technicians & Specialists	144	< 1.0
Operations & Trades	817	1.2
Sales & Customer Support	7,748	11.3
Administrative & Clerical	10,192	14.9
Service & Support	310	< 1.0
Unknown	25,321	36.9
TOTAL	68,565	100.0

As previously described, we included an approximately equal number of both selection and development cases of MVPI data in the normative data set. In addition, to account for other stratification variables of interest we included a small number of cases without a defined assessment purpose. The final distribution of cases across assessment purposes appears in Table 6.3.

Table 6.3

Norming Sample Distribution by Assessment Purpose

Assessment Purpose	Number of Cases	Percent of Final Sample
Selection	35,419	51.7
Development	31,568	46.0
Unknown	1,578	2.3
TOTAL	68,565	100.0

The final norming sample included 68,565 cases representing various occupational groups within the U.S. workforce. To guide our efforts to specify general demographic characteristics in the normative sample, we obtained population estimates from the U.S. Census Bureau's American FactFinder program. As previously described, we used population estimates collected in July 2006 to determine the percentages of various age, sex, and race/ethnicity groups in the U.S. working population. We then compared these percentages to those from the normative sample. Age, sex, and race/ethnicity distributions in the final norming sample appear below in Tables 6.4, 6.5, and 6.6, respectively. Table 6.7 provides a more detailed breakdown of age, sex, and race/ethnicity variables in the normative sample.

Table 6.4

Age Distribution of the Final Norming Sample

Age	Number of Cases	Percent of Sample	Percent in Population
Under 40	20,086	29.3	42.3
40 and Over	16,575	24.2	37.4
Not Indicated	36,661	53.5	20.3
TOTAL	68,565	100.0	100.0

As Table 6.4 indicates, the normative sample includes a proper balance of respondents across both age groups. Although we included a significant number of cases with missing age data, these cases were necessary to represent other valued occupational and demographic stratification variables. Of particular importance in this table is the fact that the rank-ordering of, and ratio between, both age groups in the normative sample are consistent with that found in the U.S. working population.

Table 6.5

Sex Distribution of the Final Norming Sample

Sex	Number of Cases	Percent of Sample	Percent in Population
Male	36,295	52.9	48.6
Female	27,391	39.9	51.4
Not Indicated	4,879	7.1	N/A
TOTAL	68,565	100.0	100.0

As displayed in Table 6.5, nearly equal numbers of males and females comprise the U.S. population. Although the normative sample included a higher percentage of cases from males, female cases still represent approximately 40% of the normative sample. We included a higher percentage of males and a significant number of cases with missing sex data to account for other valued occupational and demographic stratification variables.

Table 6.6

Race/Ethnicity Distribution of Final Norming Sample

Ethnicity	Number of Cases	Percent of Sample	Percent in Pop.
Two or More Races	10	< 1.0	1.6
Black/African American	4,718	6.9	12.8
Hispanic/Latino	5,205	7.6	14.8
Asian	3,033	4.4	4.4
American Indian/Alaska Native	541	< 1.0	1.0
White	35,794	52.2	65.2
Not Indicated	19.264	28.1	N/A
TOTAL	68,565	100.0	100.0

Note. No applicants identified themselves as Native Hawaiian or Pacific Islander

Table 6.6 illustrates that the racial and ethnic composition of the normative sample closely parallels that of the U.S. working population. We included a significant number of cases with missing race/ethnicity data to account for other valued occupational and demographic stratification variables. Excluding these cases, the ratio of percentages across groups reasonably represents the U.S. workforce. We only included 10 cases representing "Two or More Races" because more cases were not available for this group. This results from the fact that the EEOC added the official "Two or More Races" classification *after* much of these MVPI data were collected.

Descriptive Statistics of the Norming Sample

On the following pages, Tables 6.7 through 6.15 present means and standard deviations for the MVPI scales categorized by selected demographic groups. Table 6.7 provides the general structure for all following tables, presenting these data across racial and ethnic groups included in the normative sample. Table 6.8 presents these data for respondents under the age of 40, with Table 6.9 reporting scores for those 40 and over. Tables 6.10 and 6.11 follow the same pattern, presenting scores for males and females, respectively. Finally, Tables 6.12 and 6.13 present data for males and females under age 40, with Tables 6.14 and 6.15 reporting the same data for males and females age 40 and over. Total possible scores for all MVPI scales range from 20 to 60. For all tables presented, we computed statistics from the norming sample. Any specific subgroup data can be requested from Hogan. Appendix A contains raw score to percentile conversions for the total sample across all MVPI scales for the 2010 norms. For comparison purposes, Appendix B contains raw score to percentile conversions for the total sample across all MVPI scales for the 2002 norms.

Table 6.7

Norming Sample Scale Means and Standard Deviations for Racial/Ethnic Groups

Race/Ethnicity		0	1	2	3	4	5	6	TOTAL
	N	10	4,718	5,205	3,033	541	35,794	19,264	68,565
AES	M	37.80	35.39	35.54	36.43	37.00	35.00	35.54	35.30
	SD	7.97	7.76	8.05	8.19	8.36	7.93	7.76	7.90
AFF	M	49.20	49.98	51.28	50.63	50.63	50.33	49.99	50.30
	SD	4.39	4.29	3.97	5.12	4.52	4.96	5.12	4.91
ALT	M	52.00	52.35	51.60	51.28	51.67	50.41	49.79	50.51
	SD	3.40	5.13	5.56	6.13	5.61	6.07	6.44	6.12
COM	M	45.00	48.42	47.85	47.47	47.72	46.06	45.49	46.27
	SD	8.79	5.53	5.68	6.14	5.71	6.00	6.10	6.04
HED	M	39.80	37.37	38.01	40.49	37.69	38.30	38.76	38.43
	SD	7.44	6.62	6.63	6.72	6.61	6.81	6.73	6.78
POW	M	47.70	49.56	50.13	50.02	49.84	48.72	48.23	48.81
	SD	5.96	5.90	5.69	6.14	5.72	6.26	6.41	6.26
REC	M	43.00	42.64	43.29	44.98	42.29	41.53	41.12	41.78
	SD	3.83	8.02	8.01	8.13	8.16	7.96	7.86	8.00
SCI	M	42.30	40.89	42.36	43.94	43.30	41.35	40.79	41.37
	SD	9.01	7.63	7.56	7.99	7.55	7.98	8.00	7.96
SEC	M	41.20	46.02	44.61	42.41	43.01	41.46	40.39	41.76
	SD	8.83	5.93	6.16	6.78	6.62	6.98	7.16	7.07
TRA	M	47.00	49.82	47.46	46.71	48.84	48.08	47.51	47.94
	SD	6.67	5.48	5.73	5.82	6.05	6.29	6.18	6.18

Note. 0 = Two or More Races, 1 = Black or African-American, 2 = Hispanic or Latino, 3 = Asian, 4 = American Indian or Alaska Native, 5 = White, 6 = Not Indicated; AES = Aesthetic, AFF = Affiliation, ALT = Altruistic, COM = Commercial, HED = Hedonistic, POW = Power, REC = Recognition, SCI = Scientific, SEC = Security, TRA = Tradition, No applicants identified themselves as Native Hawaiian or Pacific Islander

Table 6.8

Norming Sample Scale Means and Standard Deviations for Racial/Ethnic Groups Under Age 40

Race/Ethnicity		1	2	3	4	5	6	TOTAL
	N	1,475	1,189	1,313	107	13,155	2,842	20,086
AES	M	34.85	34.53	36.17	33.88	33.91	35.42	34.38
	SD	7.46	7.35	8.07	7.63	7.57	7.77	7.64
AFF	M	50.04	50.87	50.46	50.25	50.85	50.59	50.72
	SD	4.41	4.40	5.19	5.71	4.97	5.01	4.93
ALT	M	52.51	51.06	50.81	49.42	49.89	49.30	50.13
	SD	5.11	5.88	6.46	6.25	6.31	6.46	6.28
COM	M	48.16	46.59	46.93	47.28	46.21	45.36	46.31
	SD	5.39	5.85	6.10	5.62	6.05	6.26	6.06
HED	M	37.82	38.71	41.43	39.24	39.75	40.85	39.81
	SD	6.75	6.64	6.86	6.55	6.92	6.63	6.89
POW	M	49.12	49.28	49.70	49.68	49.18	48.72	49.15
	SD	6.12	6.05	6.00	5.89	6.15	6.43	6.18
REC	M	41.75	41.91	45.42	41.62	42.24	42.71	42.45
	SD	8.14	7.95	7.88	7.76	7.94	7.77	7.97
SCI	M	41.11	42.03	43.81	41.82	41.91	41.51	41.93
	SD	7.64	7.75	8.28	8.93	8.20	8.37	8.18
SEC	M	45.24	43.19	41.65	41.42	40.95	39.91	41.30
	SD	6.07	6.66	7.10	7.26	7.00	7.29	7.09
TRA	M	50.07	47.62	46.31	49.62	47.71	46.20	47.58
	SD	5.31	5.76	5.68	6.18	6.40	6.42	6.32

Note. Two or More Races is not reported due to insufficient sample size (N = 5); 1 = Black or African-American, 2 = Hispanic or Latino, 3 = Asian, 4 = American Indian or Alaska Native, 5 = White, 6 = Not Indicated; AES = Aesthetic, AFF = Affiliation, ALT = Altruistic, COM = Commercial, HED = Hedonistic, POW = Power, REC = Recognition, SCI = Scientific, SEC = Security, TRA = Tradition, No applicants identified themselves as Native Hawaiian or Pacific Islander

Table 6.9

Norming Sample Scale Means and Standard Deviations for Racial/Ethnic Groups Age 40 and Over

Race/Ethnicity		1	2	3	4	5	6	TOTAL
	N	693	514	574	97	12,063	2,630	*16,575*
AES	*M*	35.75	35.04	35.90	34.49	35.04	36.02	35.26
	SD	7.75	7.74	8.38	7.47	7.80	7.85	7.83
AFF	*M*	48.50	49.46	48.91	48.78	48.86	48.96	48.88
	SD	4.69	4.66	5.91	4.60	5.36	5.41	5.34
ALT	*M*	51.69	49.72	50.51	49.76	49.46	48.77	49.49
	SD	5.32	6.48	6.50	6.82	6.24	6.60	6.31
COM	*M*	46.22	45.57	45.60	45.33	44.60	44.14	44.67
	SD	5.73	5.80	6.35	5.95	6.11	6.39	6.15
HED	*M*	36.56	37.44	39.23	36.11	37.06	38.20	37.30
	SD	6.51	6.43	6.59	6.82	6.62	6.54	6.62
POW	*M*	47.66	47.99	48.70	48.18	46.99	46.93	47.11
	SD	6.53	6.32	7.00	6.38	6.59	6.87	6.65
REC	*M*	40.19	40.20	42.13	37.91	39.24	39.92	39.51
	SD	8.06	8.08	8.88	8.00	7.73	7.74	7.82
SCI	*M*	39.07	40.58	42.37	41.87	40.08	40.19	40.16
	SD	7.56	7.65	8.26	7.38	8.04	8.15	8.04
SEC	*M*	43.98	42.40	41.60	40.40	39.92	39.29	40.13
	SD	7.01	7.63	7.09	6.78	7.14	7.37	7.25
TRA	*M*	50.84	48.57	47.66	49.06	48.62	47.22	48.46
	SD	5.26	5.78	5.90	6.91	6.33	6.25	6.29

Note. Two or More Races is not reported due to insufficient sample size (N = 4); 1 = Black or African-American, 2 = Hispanic or Latino, 3 = Asian, 4 = American Indian or Alaska Native, 5 = White, 6 = Not Indicated; AES = Aesthetic, AFF = Affiliation, ALT = Altruistic, COM = Commercial, HED = Hedonistic, POW = Power, REC = Recognition, SCI = Scientific, SEC = Security, TRA = Tradition, No applicants identified themselves as Native Hawaiian or Pacific Islander

Table 6.10

Norming Sample Scale Means and Standard Deviations for Racial/Ethnic Groups by Males

Race/Ethnicity		1	2	3	4	5	6	TOTAL
	N	2,457	3,301	1.998	335	19,828	8,371	36,295
AES	M	35.21	35.18	35.57	36.00	33.86	34.55	34.34
	SD	7.79	8.00	8.10	8.30	7.61	7.54	7.70
AFF	M	50.28	51.35	50.73	50.72	50.05	49.79	50.17
	SD	4.25	3.98	5.17	4.77	5.18	5.31	5.07
ALT	M	52.22	51.17	51.11	51.04	49.42	48.89	49.75
	SD	5.20	5.65	6.34	5.87	6.29	6.60	6.31
COM	M	49.30	48.49	48.47	48.21	46.95	46.48	47.24
	SD	5.18	5.47	5.81	5.51	5.76	5.77	5.76
HED	M	37.33	38.03	40.12	37.43	37.91	38.50	38.14
	SD	6.58	6.53	6.68	6.58	6.78	6.68	6.74
POW	M	50.40	50.58	50.81	50.09	49.39	49.08	49.58
	SD	5.63	5.43	5.84	5.78	6.01	6.17	5.98
REC	M	42.94	43.64	45.35	42.18	41.42	41.39	41.94
	SD	8.10	8.05	8.23	8.22	8.09	8.05	8.16
SCI	M	42.05	43.13	45.28	44.05	42.48	42.02	42.57
	SD	7.36	7.33	7.61	7.23	7.83	7.94	7.80
SEC	M	45.88	44.39	42.58	42.70	40.93	39.96	41.46
	SD	5.99	6.30	6.75	6.71	7.06	7.23	7.15
TRA	M	50.17	47.57	46.78	48.93	48.29	47.47	48.09
	SD	5.36	5.64	5.83	6.34	6.46	6.38	6.31

Note. Two or More Races is not reported due to insufficient sample size (N = 5); 1 = Black or African-American, 2 = Hispanic or Latino, 3 = Asian, 4 = American Indian or Alaska Native, 5 = White, 6 = Not Indicated; AES = Aesthetic, AFF = Affiliation, ALT = Altruistic, COM = Commercial, HED = Hedonistic, POW = Power, REC = Recognition, SCI = Scientific, SEC = Security, TRA = Tradition, No applicants identified themselves as Native Hawaiian or Pacific Islander

Table 6.11

Norming Sample Scale Means and Standard Deviations for Racial/Ethnic Groups by Females

Race/Ethnicity		1	2	3	4	5	6	TOTAL
	N	2,218	1,880	964	201	15,571	6.552	27,391
AES	M	35.60	36.17	38.23	38.74	36.45	36.82	36.53
	SD	7.74	8.11	8.10	8.22	8.09	7.82	8.01
AFF	M	49.66	51.19	50.57	50.53	50.72	50.50	50.61
	SD	4.30	3.90	4.95	4.07	4.64	4.78	4.62
ALT	M	52.55	52.38	51.80	52.81	51.70	51.22	51.71
	SD	4.99	5.27	5.63	4.90	5.52	5.91	5.57
COM	M	47.44	46.75	45.64	46.97	44.92	44.17	45.11
	SD	5.73	5.87	6.27	6.01	6.11	6.12	6.14
HED	M	37.44	37.98	41.42	38.18	38.81	39.59	38.92
	SD	6.64	6.82	6.71	6.61	6.83	6.66	6.81
POW	M	48.67	49.37	48.66	49.44	47.88	47.24	47.93
	SD	6.05	6.04	6.31	5.58	6.48	6.49	6.43
REC	M	42.32	42.71	44.39	42.69	41.68	41.14	41.78
	SD	7.89	7.89	7.92	8.03	7.78	7.55	7.78
SCI	M	39.63	41.03	41.33	42.01	39.93	38.99	39.82
	SD	7.72	7.76	8.13	7.98	7.94	7.74	7.89
SEC	M	46.22	45.01	42.23	43.60	42.16	40.91	42.40
	SD	5.85	5.86	6.75	6.49	6.82	7.04	6.90
TRA	M	49.44	47.25	46.66	48.73	47.81	47.59	47.82
	SD	5.60	5.88	5.76	5.59	6.05	5.87	5.97

Note. Two or More Races is not reported due to insufficient sample size (N = 5); 1 = Black or African-American, 2 = Hispanic or Latino, 3 = Asian, 4 = American Indian or Alaska Native, 5 = White, 6 = Not Indicated; AES = Aesthetic, AFF = Affiliation, ALT = Altruistic, COM = Commercial, HED = Hedonistic, POW = Power, REC = Recognition, SCI = Scientific, SEC = Security, TRA = Tradition, No applicants identified themselves as Native Hawaiian or Pacific Islander

Compilation of Norms

Table 6.12

Norming Sample Scale Means and Standard Deviations for Racial/Ethnic Groups by Males Under 40

Race/Ethnicity		1	2	3	4	5	6	TOTAL
	N	805	724	838	72	7,781	1,598	11,821
AES	M	34.59	33.89	35.17	32.15	32.94	34.38	33.46
	SD	7.61	7.28	7.90	6.68	7.21	7.52	7.37
AFF	M	50.43	51.05	50.39	50.33	50.71	50.59	50.67
	SD	4.36	4.42	5.34	5.96	5.03	5.01	4.98
ALT	M	52.20	50.47	50.53	49.13	49.09	48.39	49.40
	SD	5.28	6.08	6.76	6.62	6.40	6.79	6.46
COM	M	49.24	47.30	47.98	47.71	47.42	46.73	47.49
	SD	4.99	5.63	5.82	5.57	5.70	5.83	5.70
HED	M	37.63	38.54	40.82	39.14	39.21	40.33	39.32
	SD	6.71	6.57	6.79	6.13	6.89	6.59	6.84
POW	M	50.22	50.19	50.43	50.28	50.05	49.87	50.08
	SD	5.70	5.56	5.74	5.62	5.78	6.02	5.79
REC	M	42.15	42.12	45.76	41.51	42.24	43.15	42.60
	SD	8.23	8.01	8.04	7.17	8.04	7.73	8.06
SCI	M	42.52	43.32	45.52	42.74	43.37	43.38	43.46
	SD	7.43	7.39	7.70	8.12	7.89	7.91	7.84
SEC	M	45.20	42.69	41.55	41.44	40.56	39.52	40.94
	SD	6.14	6.89	7.15	7.34	7.05	7.31	7.15
TRA	M	50.29	47.72	46.31	49.99	47.93	46.08	47.73
	SD	5.29	5.86	5.73	6.38	6.54	6.64	6.46

Note. Two or More Races is not reported due to insufficient sample size (N = 3); 1 = Black or African-American, 2 = Hispanic or Latino, 3 = Asian, 4 = American Indian or Alaska Native, 5 = White, 6 = Not Indicated; AES = Aesthetic, AFF = Affiliation, ALT = Altruistic, COM = Commercial, HED = Hedonistic, POW = Power, REC = Recognition, SCI = Scientific, SEC = Security, TRA = Tradition, No applicants identified themselves as Native Hawaiian or Pacific Islander

Table 6.13

Norming Sample Scale Means and Standard Deviations for Racial/Ethnic Groups by Females Under 40

Race/Ethnicity		1	2	3	4	5	6	TOTAL
	N	668	464	474	35	5,361	1,216	8,220
AES	M	35.17	35.54	37.96	37.43	35.32	36.79	35.70
	SD	7.26	7.36	8.06	8.32	7.84	7.88	7.83
AFF	M	49.58	50.59	50.57	50.09	51.05	50.56	50.80
	SD	4.43	4.36	4.92	5.24	4.87	5.03	4.85
ALT	M	52.90	51.98	51.30	50.03	51.06	50.49	51.18
	SD	4.84	5.44	5.87	5.45	5.99	5.81	5.87
COM	M	46.88	45.48	45.07	46.40	44.44	43.53	44.61
	SD	5.55	6.03	6.16	5.70	6.12	6.35	6.16
HED	M	38.06	38.97	42.51	39.46	40.55	41.50	40.51
	SD	6.79	6.75	6.84	7.43	6.89	6.64	6.91
POW	M	47.81	47.84	48.41	48.46	47.92	47.19	47.83
	SD	6.33	6.49	6.24	6.33	6.46	6.66	6.47
REC	M	41.28	41.58	44.81	41.83	42.22	42.12	42.24
	SD	8.01	7.85	7.56	8.98	7.81	7.79	7.84
SCI	M	39.45	40.03	40.78	39.94	39.79	39.09	39.73
	SD	7.55	7.87	8.41	10.26	8.17	8.36	8.16
SEC	M	45.28	43.98	41.82	41.37	41.52	40.37	41.81
	SD	5.99	6.21	7.03	7.21	6.89	7.25	6.97
TRA	M	49.82	47.44	46.30	48.86	47.39	46.31	47.37
	SD	5.32	5.59	5.60	5.77	6.18	6.12	6.10

Note. Two or More Races is not reported due to insufficient sample size (N = 2); 1 = Black or African-American, 2 = Hispanic or Latino, 3 = Asian, 4 = American Indian or Alaska Native, 5 = White, 6 = Not Indicated; AES = Aesthetic, AFF = Affiliation, ALT = Altruistic, COM = Commercial, HED = Hedonistic, POW = Power, REC = Recognition, SCI = Scientific, SEC = Security, TRA = Tradition, No applicants identified themselves as Native Hawaiian or Pacific Islander

Compilation of Norms

Table 6.14

Norming Sample Scale Means and Standard Deviations for Racial/Ethnic Groups by Males 40 & Over

Race/Ethnicity		1	2	3	4	5	6	TOTAL
	N	402	359	410	68	7,820	1,725	10,786
AES	M	34.75	33.95	34.75	34.07	33.95	34.99	34.18
	SD	7.63	7.37	8.08	7.36	7.54	7.55	7.57
AFF	M	48.76	49.35	49.05	49.41	48.65	48.75	48.72
	SD	4.51	4.90	6.10	4.65	5.54	5.69	5.53
ALT	M	51.56	49.15	50.00	49.25	48.68	47.98	48.74
	SD	5.33	6.37	6.74	7.14	6.41	6.69	6.47
COM	M	47.07	46.19	46.47	46.10	45.65	45.16	45.67
	SD	5.66	5.77	6.26	6.29	5.86	6.08	5.91
HED	M	36.04	37.04	39.03	35.81	36.72	38.12	37.01
	SD	6.31	6.33	6.64	7.23	6.56	6.62	6.60
POW	M	48.44	48.70	49.45	48.46	47.94	47.81	48.03
	SD	6.38	6.19	6.90	6.42	6.31	6.75	6.41
REC	M	40.05	40.48	42.50	38.43	39.44	40.22	39.74
	SD	8.29	8.25	9.13	8.38	7.90	7.90	8.00
SCI	M	40.70	41.08	43.50	42.59	41.13	41.35	41.24
	SD	7.25	7.63	8.11	7.41	7.93	8.10	7.94
SEC	M	44.17	42.11	41.53	40.47	39.74	39.24	39.97
	SD	7.05	7.76	7.05	6.75	7.10	7.26	7.21
TRA	M	50.80	48.56	47.28	49.59	48.73	47.08	48.49
	SD	5.22	5.76	6.01	7.09	6.51	6.41	6.46

Note. Two or More Races is not reported due to insufficient sample size (N = 2); 1 = Black or African-American, 2 = Hispanic or Latino, 3 = Asian, 4 = American Indian or Alaska Native, 5 = White, 6 = Not Indicated; AES = Aesthetic, AFF = Affiliation, ALT = Altruistic, COM = Commercial, HED = Hedonistic, POW = Power, REC = Recognition, SCI = Scientific, SEC = Security, TRA = Tradition, No applicants identified themselves as Native Hawaiian or Pacific Islander

Table 6.15

Norming Sample Scale Means and Standard Deviations for Racial/Ethnic Groups Females 40 & Over

Race/Ethnicity		1	2	3	4	5	6	TOTAL
	N	*289*	*154*	*162*	*27*	*4,216*	*876*	*5,726*
AES	*M*	37.17	37.56	38.80	35.74	37.07	38.07	37.28
	SD	7.70	8.03	8.49	7.82	7.87	8.09	7.93
AFF	*M*	48.11	49.71	48.51	47.56	49.25	49.38	49.19
	SD	4.90	4.07	5.43	4.23	4.99	4.82	4.96
ALT	*M*	51.93	51.16	51.87	50.96	50.92	50.25	50.90
	SD	5.28	6.39	5.67	5.86	5.64	6.19	5.74
COM	*M*	45.03	44.11	43.43	43.33	42.67	42.10	42.76
	SD	5.62	5.64	6.11	4.66	6.09	6.54	6.16
HED	*M*	37.29	38.34	39.76	36.96	37.69	38.41	37.85
	SD	6.72	6.58	6.44	5.67	6.69	6.37	6.64
POW	*M*	46.57	46.32	46.91	47.04	45.21	45.21	45.37
	SD	6.59	6.36	6.88	6.10	6.72	6.82	6.74
REC	*M*	40.37	39.46	41.13	36.78	38.85	39.26	39.06
	SD	7.74	7.58	8.18	7.24	7.38	7.39	7.44
SCI	*M*	36.84	39.47	39.51	39.59	38.13	37.86	38.11
	SD	7.39	7.58	7.99	7.07	7.87	7.70	7.82
SEC	*M*	43.77	43.10	41.88	40.37	40.28	39.29	40.42
	SD	6.95	7.31	7.17	7.18	7.21	7.53	7.31
TRA	*M*	50.90	48.62	48.59	47.74	48.44	47.43	48.42
	SD	5.33	5.87	5.55	6.60	5.98	5.91	5.97

Note. Two or More Races is not reported due to insufficient sample size (N = 2); 1 = Black or African-American, 2 = Hispanic or Latino, 3 = Asian, 4 = American Indian or Alaska Native, 5 = White, 6 = Not Indicated; AES = Aesthetic, AFF = Affiliation, ALT = Altruistic, COM = Commercial, HED = Hedonistic, POW = Power, REC = Recognition, SCI = Scientific, SEC = Security, TRA = Tradition, No applicants identified themselves as Native Hawaiian or Pacific Islander

Appendix A: 2010 MVPI NORMS (N=68,565)

SCORE	AESTHETIC	AFFILIATION	ALTRUISTIC	COMMERCIAL	HEDONISTIC	POWER	RECOGNITION	SCIENTIFIC	SECURITY	TRADITION
0-19										
20	0	0	0	0	0	0	0	0	0	0
21	1	0	0	0	0	0	0	0	0	0
22	2	0	0	0	0	0	0	0	0	0
23	3	0	0	0	1	0	1	1	0	0
24	6	0	0	0	1	0	1	1	1	0
25	8	0	0	0	2	0	2	2	1	0
26	13	0	0	0	4	0	3	3	2	0
27	17	0	0	0	5	0	4	4	3	0
28	22	0	0	0	8	0	6	6	4	0
29	27	0	0	1	10	0	7	7	5	0
30	32	0	0	1	13	1	9	10	7	0
31	37	0	1	2	16	1	11	12	9	1
32	42	1	1	2	21	1	14	15	12	1
33	46	1	1	3	25	2	16	18	14	1
34	51	1	2	4	30	2	20	22	17	2
35	55	1	2	5	34	3	22	25	20	3
36	60	2	3	7	41	4	27	29	24	4
37	63	2	3	9	45	5	30	32	27	5
38	68	3	5	11	51	7	35	37	32	7
39	71	3	5	14	56	8	38	40	36	9
40	74	4	7	17	62	11	44	45	41	12
41	77	5	9	21	66	13	48	49	45	15
42	80	7	11	26	72	16	53	54	51	20
43	83	8	13	30	75	19	57	58	55	23
44	86	11	16	36	81	24	62	63	61	29
45	88	13	19	41	84	27	66	67	66	34
46	90	19	24	48	87	33	71	72	72	40
47	92	22	27	54	90	37	74	75	76	45
48	93	31	33	61	93	44	79	80	82	52
49	95	36	38	67	94	49	81	83	86	57
50	96	48	44	74	96	57	85	87	90	64
51	97	55	50	79	97	62	87	89	93	69
52	98	67	58	86	99	69	91	92	96	75
53	98	73	64	89	99	74	92	94	97	79
54	99	83	72	94	100	81	95	96	99	85
55	99	87	77	96	100	85	96	97	99	88
56	100	93	84	98	100	91	98	98	100	93
57	100	95	88	99	100	94	98	99	100	95
58	100	98	94	100	100	98	99	100	100	98
59	100	99	96	100	100	99	100	100	100	98
60	100	100	100	100	100	100	100	100	100	100

Appendix B: 2002 MVPI NORMS (N=10,000)

SCORE	AESTHETIC	AFFILIATION	ALTRUISTIC	COMMERCIAL	HEDONISTIC	POWER	RECOGNITION	SCIENTIFIC	SECURITY	TRADITION
0-19										
20	1	0	0	0	0	0	0	0	0	0
21	1	0	0	0	0	0	0	0	0	0
22	3	0	0	0	1	0	0	0	0	0
23	4	0	0	0	1	0	0	1	0	0
24	8	0	0	0	2	0	0	1	0	0
25	10	0	0	0	2	0	0	2	1	0
26	16	0	0	1	4	0	1	3	1	0
27	20	0	1	1	6	0	1	4	1	1
28	26	0	1	1	8	0	2	7	2	1
29	31	1	1	1	10	1	3	9	3	1
30	38	1	1	2	14	1	4	12	4	2
31	43	1	1	3	17	1	5	14	5	2
32	48	1	1	4	23	2	8	18	7	3
33	52	1	2	5	27	2	9	21	8	4
34	57	2	2	7	33	2	12	25	11	5
35	60	3	2	9	37	3	15	28	13	6
36	64	3	3	12	44	4	20	33	16	8
37	68	4	4	14	48	6	22	37	19	11
38	72	5	5	18	54	8	28	42	24	14
39	75	6	6	22	59	9	31	45	27	17
40	78	8	8	27	66	12	36	51	33	21
41	80	9	10	31	70	15	40	55	37	25
42	83	12	12	38	74	20	46	60	43	30
43	85	15	14	42	77	24	50	65	47	34
44	88	19	17	49	82	28	56	70	55	40
45	89	22	20	53	85	33	61	74	60	44
46	91	27	24	59	89	40	66	79	67	50
47	92	32	27	64	90	45	70	82	72	54
48	93	40	32	70	93	54	75	86	80	59
49	95	46	37	75	94	60	79	88	84	63
50	96	56	43	81	96	67	84	91	90	69
51	96	62	48	85	98	72	87	93	92	73
52	97	73	55	90	99	79	91	95	96	78
53	98	78	60	93	99	83	92	96	97	82
54	98	87	68	96	99	88	95	97	99	87
55	99	90	73	97	100	91	96	98	99	89
56	99	96	80	99	100	95	98	99	100	92
57	99	97	85	99	100	97	99	99	100	94
58	100	99	93	100	100	99	100	100	100	97
59	100	100	96	100	100	100	100	100	100	98
60	100	100	100	100	100	100	100	100	100	100

References

Abrahams, N. M., & Neumann, I. (1973). Predicting the unpredictable: A validation of the Strong Vocational Interest Blank for predicting military aptitude ratings of Naval Academy midshipmen. *Proceedings of the 81st Annual Convention of the American Psychological Association, 8*(2), 747-748.

ACT, Inc. (1981). *Technical report for the unisex edition of the ACT Interest Inventory (UNIACT).* Iowa City, IA: Author.

Allport, G. W. (1961). *Pattern and growth in personality.* New York: Holt, Rinehart, and Winston.

Allport, G. W., Vernon, P. E., & Lindzey, G. (1960). *Study of values* (3rd ed.). Boston: Houghton-Mifflin.

American Educational Research Association, American Psychological Association, and the National Council on Measurement in Education. (1999). *Standards for educational and psychological testing.* Washington, DC: American Educational Research Association.

Americans With Disabilities Act of 1990, 102(b)(7), 42 U.S.C.A. 12112.

American Psychiatric Association. (1994). *Diagnostic and statistical manual of mental disorders* (4th ed.). Washington, DC: Author.

Barak, A., & Meir, E. I. (1974). The predictive validity of a vocational interest inventory—"RAMAK": Seven year follow-up. *Journal of Vocational Behavior, 4,* 377-387.

Barge, B. N., & Hough, L. M. (1988). Utility of interest assessment for predicting job performance. In L. M. Hough, *Utility of temperament, biodata, and interest assessment for predicting job performance* (ARI Research Note 88-02). Alexandria, VA: U.S. Army Research Institute for the Behavioral and Social Sciences.

Barron, F. X. (1965). The psychology of creativity. In D. Cartwright (Ed.), *New Directions in Psychology II* (pp. 1-134). New York: Holt, Rinehart, & Winston.

Bartling, H. C., & Hood, A. B. (1981). An 11-year follow-up of measured interest and vocational choice. *Journal of Counseling Psychology, 28,* 27-35.

Bordin, E. S. (1943). A theory of vocational interests as dynamic phenomena. *Educational and Psychological Measurement, 3,* 49-65.

Borgen, F. H., Weiss, D. J., Tinsley, H. E. A., Dawis, R. V., & Lofquist, L. H. (1968). *Occupational Reinforcer Patterns* (Minnesota Studies in Vocational Rehabilitation XXIV). Minneapolis: Industrial Relations Center, University of Minnesota.

Borman, W. C., Toquam, J. L., & Rosse, R. L. (1979). *Development and validation of an inventory battery to predict Navy and Marine Corps recruiter performance* (Technical Report No. 22). Minneapolis, MN: Personnel Decisions Research Institute.

Brandt, J. E., & Hood, A. B. (1968). Effect of personality adjustment on the predictive validity of the Strong Vocational Interest Blank. *Journal of Counseling Psychology, 15,* 547-551.

Burke, M. J., Brief, A. P., & George, J. M. (1993). The role negative affectivity in understanding relations between self-reports of stressors and strains: A comment on applied psychology literature. *Journal of Applied Psychology, 78,* 402-412.

Butler, F. J., Crinnion, J., & Martin, J. (1972). The Kuder Preference Record in adult vocational guidance. *Occupational Psychology, 46,* 99-104.

Cairo, P. C. (1982). Measured interests versus expressed interests as predictors of long-term occupational membership. *Journal of Vocational Behavior, 20,* 343-353.

Campbell, D. P. (1966). Occupations ten years later of high school seniors with high scores on the SVIB Life Insurance Salesman scale. *Journal of Applied Psychology, 50,* 51-56.

Campbell, D. P. (1971). *Handbook for the Strong Vocational Interest Blank.* Stanford, CA: Stanford University Press.

Campbell, D. P., & Holland, J. L. (1972). Applying Holland's theory to Strong's data. *Journal of Vocational Behavior, 2,* 353-376.

Campbell, D. T. (1963). Social attitudes and other acquired behavioral dispositions. In S. Koch (Ed.), *Psychology: A study of a science.* New York: McGraw-Hill.

Clark, K. E. (1961). *Vocational interests of non-professional men.* Minneapolis, MN: University of Minnesota Press.

Costa, P. T., & McCrae, R. R. (1980). Influence of extraversion and neuroticism on subjective wellbeing: Happy and unhappy people. *Journal of Personality and Social Psychology, 38,* 668-678.

Cronbach, L. J. (1951). Coefficient alpha and the internal structure of tests. *Psychometrika, 16,* 297334.

Cronbach, L. J. (1984). *Essentials of psychological testing* (4th ed.). New York: Harper & Row.

Dann, J. E., & Abrahams, N. M. (1977). *Occupational scales of the Navy Vocational Interest Inventory: III. Relationship to job satisfaction, "A" school grades, and job performance* (Technical Report No. 783). San Diego, CA: Navy Personnel Research and Development Center.

Darley, J. B., & Hagenah, T. (1955). *Vocational interest measurement: Theory and practice.* Minneapolis, MN: University of Minnesota Press.

Dawis, R. V. (1980). Measuring interests. *New directions in testing and measurement, 7,* 77-91.

Dawis, R. V., Dohm, T. E., Lofquist, L. H., Chartrand, J. M., & Due, A. M. (1987). *Minnesota Occupational Classification System III.* Minneapolis, MN: Vocational Psychology Research, Department of Psychology, University of Minnesota.

Dawis, R. V., & Lofquist, L. H. (1984). *A psychological theory of work adjustment.* Minneapolis, MN: University of Minnesota Press.

Dawis, R.V. (1991). Vocational interests, values, and preferences. In M. D. Dunnette & L. M.
Hough (Eds.). *Handbook of industrial and organizational psychology* (pp. 833-871).
Palo Alto, CA: Consulting Psychologists Press.

DeMichael, S. G., & Dabelstein, D. H. (1947). Work satisfaction and work efficiency of
vocational rehabilitation counselors as related to measured interests (Abstract).
American Psychologist, 2, 342-343.

Dolliver, R. H., Irvin, J. A., & Bigley, S. S. (1972). Twelve-year follow-up of the Strong
Vocational Interest Blank. *Journal of Counseling Psychology, 19,* 212-217.

Dolliver, R. H., & Will, J. A. (1977). Ten-year follow-up of the Tyler Vocational Card Sort and
the Strong Vocational Interest Blank. *Journal of Counseling Psychology, 24,* 48-54.

Dunnette, M. D., & Aylward, M. S. (1956). Validity information exchange, No. 9-21. *Personnel
Psychology, 9,* 245-247.

Equal Employment Opportunity Commission, Civil Service Commission, Department of Labor,
& Department of Justice. (1978). Uniform guidelines on employee selection
procedures. *Federal Register, 43,* 38290-38315

Equal Employment Opportunity Commission, Office of Management and Budget. (2006).
Section 15: Race and Color Discrimination. *EEOC Compliance manual.* Washington,
DC: Government Printing Office.

Feltham, R., & Loan-Clarke, J. (2007). Hogan's Motives, Values, Preferences Inventory
(MVPI). In P. A. Lindley (Ed.), *British Psychological Society Psychological Testing
Centre test reviews.* London: British Psychological Society.

Gade, E. M., & Soliah, D. (1975). Vocational preference inventory high point codes versus
expressed choices as predictors of college major and career entry. *Journal of
Counseling Psychology, 22,* 117-121.

Gati, I. (1991). The structure of vocational interests. *Psychological Bulletin, 109,* 309-324.

Goldberg, L. R. (1992). The development of markers for the big-five factor structure. *Psychological Assessment, 4,* 26-42.

Gregory, W. S. (1992). *Construct validity of personal motives.* Unpublished doctoral dissertation, University of Tulsa, Tulsa, OK.

Guilford, J. P., Christiansen, P. R., Bond, N. A., Jr., & Sutton, M. A. (1954). A factor analysis study of human interest. *Psychological Monographs, 68,* 38.

Hahn, M. E., & Williams, C. T. (1945). The measured interest of Marine Corps women reservists. *Journal of Applied Psychology, 29,* 198-211.

Hansen, J. C. (1984). The measurement of vocational interests: Issues and future directions. In S. D. Brown & R. W. Lent (Eds.), *Handbook of Counseling Psychology* (pp. 99-136). New York: Wiley.

Hansen, J. C. (1986). *12-year longitudinal study of the predictive validity of the SVIB-SCII.* Paper presented at the 94th annual meeting of the American Psychological Association, Washington, DC.

Hansen, J. C., & Johansson, C. B. (1972). The application of Holland's vocational model to the Strong Vocational Interest Blank for Women. *Journal of Vocational Behavior, 2,* 479-493.

Hansen, J. C., & Swanson, J. L. (1983). Stability of vocational interests of adolescents and young adults. *Measurement and Evaluation in Guidance, 13,* 173-178.

Harrington, T. F., & O'Shea, A. J. (1982). *The Harrington-O'Shea Career Decision-Making System manual.* Circle Pines, MN: American Guidance Service.

Hathaway, S. R., & McKinley, J. C. (1943). *Manual for the Minnesota Multiphasic Personality Inventory.* New York: Psychological Corporation.

Herzberg, F., & Russell, D. (1953). The effects of experience and change of job interest on the Kuder Preference Record. *Journal of Applied Psychology, 37,* 478-481.

Hofstee, W. K. B. (1990). The use of everyday personality language for scientific purposes. *European Journal of Personality, 4,* 77-88.

Hogan, J., & Hogan, R. (1996). *Motives, Values, Preferences Inventory manual.* Tulsa, OK: Hogan Assessment Systems.

Hogan, R. (1983). Socioanalytic theory of personality. In M. M. Page (Ed.), *1982 Nebraska Symposium on Motivation: Personality—current theory and research* (pp. 55-89). Lincoln: University of Nebraska Press.

Hogan, R. (1995). A socioanalytic perspective on the Five-Factor Model. In J. S. Wiggins (Ed.), *Theories of the Five-Factor Model.* New York: Guilford.

Hogan, R. & Blake R. (1996). Vocational interests: Matching self-concept with the work environment. In K.R. Murphy (Ed.), *Behavior in organizations* (pp. 89-144). San Francisco: Jossey-Bass.

Hogan, R., & Hogan, J. (1995). *Hogan Personality Inventory manual.* Tulsa, OK: Hogan Assessment Systems.

Hogan, R., & Hogan, J. (1997). *Hogan Development Survey manual.* Tulsa, OK: Hogan Assessment Systems.

Hogan, R., & Hogan, J. (2007). *Hogan Personality Inventory manual.* Tulsa, OK: Hogan Assessment Systems.

Hogan, R., & Hogan, J. (2009). *Hogan Development Survey manual.* Tulsa, OK: Hogan Assessment Systems.

Hogan, R., Hogan, J., & Warrenfeltz, R. (2007). *Hogan guide.* Tulsa, OK: Hogan Assessment Systems.

Holland, J. L. (1965). *Manual: Vocational Preference Inventory.* Palo Alto, CA: Consulting Psychologists Press.

Holland, J. L. (1966). *The psychology of vocational choice: A theory of personality types and model environments.* Waltham, MA: Ginn.

Holland, J. L. (1973). *Making vocational choices: A theory of careers.* Englewood Cliffs, NJ: Prentice Hall.

Holland, J. L. (1976). Vocational preferences. In M. D. Dunnette (Ed.), *Handbook of industrial and organizational psychology* (pp. 521-570). New York: Wiley.

Holland, J. L. (1985a). *Making vocational choices: A theory of vocational personalities and work environments* (2nd ed.). Englewood Cliffs, NJ: Prentice-Hall.

Holland, J. L. (1985b). *The Self-Directed Search: Professional manual.* Odessa, FL: Psychological Assessment Resources, Inc.

Holland, J. L. (1987). *1987 manual supplement for the Self-Directed Search.* Odessa, FL: Psychological Assessment Resources.

Jackson, D. N. (1977). *Jackson Vocational Interest Survey manual.* Port Huron, MI: Research Psychologists Press.

Johansson, C. B. (1986). *Manual for the Career Assessment Inventory* (2nd ed.). Minneapolis, MN: National Computer Systems.

John, O. P. (1990). The "Big Five" factor taxonomy: Dimensions of personality in the natural language and in questionnaires. In L. Pervin (Ed.), *Handbook of personality theory and research* (pp. 66-100). New York: Guilford.

Johnson, J. C., & Dunnette, M. D. (1968). Validity and test-retest stability of the Nash managerial effectiveness scale on the revised form of the Strong Vocational Interest Blank. *Personnel Psychology, 21,* 283-294.

Jung, C. G. (1923). *Psychological types.* New York: Harcourt, Brace, Jovanovich.

Katzell, R. A. (1964). Personal values, job satisfaction, and job behavior. In H. Borow (Ed.), *Man in a world of work.* Boston: Houghton Mifflin.

Klein, K. L., & Weiner, Y. (1977). Interest congruency as a moderator of the relationships between job tenure and job satisfaction and mental health. *Journal of Vocational Behavior, 10,* 92-98.

Klinger, E. (1977). *Meaning and void: Inner experiences and the incentives in peoples' lives.* Minneapolis, MN: University of Minnesota Press.

Knauft, E. B. (1951). Vocational interests and managerial success. *Journal of Applied Psychology, 35,* 160-163.

Lau, A. W., & Abrahams, N. M. (1970). *The Navy Vocational Interest Inventory as a predictor of job performance* (Research Report SSR 70-28). San Diego, CA: Navy Personnel and Training Research Laboratory.

Lau, A. W., & Abrahams, N. M. (1971). *Reliability and predictive validity of the Navy Vocational Interest Inventory.* (Research Report SSR 71-16). San Diego, CA: Navy Personnel and Training Research Laboratory.

Layton, W. L. (1958). *Counseling use of the Strong Vocational Interest Blank.* Oxford, England: University of Minnesota Press.

Levin, I., & Stokes, J. P. (1989). Dispositional approach to job satisfaction: Role of negative affectivity. *Journal of Applied Psychology, 74,* 752-758.

Lindemann, B., & Grossman, P. (1996). *Employment discrimination law* (3rd ed.). Washington, DC: American Bar Association.

Maslow, A. H. (1954). *Motivation and personality.* New York: HarperCollins.

McArthur, C. (1954). Long-term validity of the Strong Interest Test in two subcultures. *Journal of Applied Psychology, 38,* 184-189.

McRae, G. G. (1959). *The relationship of job satisfaction and earlier measured interests.* Unpublished doctoral dissertation, University of Florida.

Meehl, P. E. (1986). Trait language and behaviorese. In T. Thompson & M. D. Zeiler (Eds.), *Analysis and integration of behavioral units* (pp. 315-334). Hillsdale, NJ: Erlbaum.

Miner, J. B. (1960). The Kuder Preference Record in managerial appraisal. *Personnel Psychology, 13,* 187-196.

Murray, H. A. (1938). *Explorations in personality: A clinical and experimental study of fifty men of college age.* New York: Oxford University Press.

Myers, I. B., & McCaulley, M. H. (1985). *Manual: A guide to the development and use of the Myers-Briggs Type Indicator.* Palo Alto, CA: Consulting Psychologists Press.

Nash, A. N. (1966). Development of an SVIB key for selecting managers. *Journal of Applied Psychology, 50,* 250-254.

North, R. D., Jr. (1958). Tests for the accounting profession. *Educational and Psychological Measurement, 18,* 691-713.

Novacek, J., & Lazarus, R. S. (1990). The structure of personal commitments. *Journal of Personality, 58,* 693-715.

Nunnally, J. C. (1967). *Psychometric theory.* New York: McGraw-Hill.

Perry, R. B. (1954). *Realms of value: A critique of human civilization.* Cambridge, MA: Harvard University Press.

Peters, R. S. (1958). *The concept of motivation.* London: Blackwell.

Pfeffer, J. (1983). Organizational demography. In L. L. Cummings & B. M. Staw (Eds.), *Research in Organizational Behavior* (Vol. 5, pp. 299-357). Greenwich, CT: JAI Press.

Psychological Corporation. (1989). *Industrial Reading Test manual.* San Antonio, TX: Author.

Roberts, B. (2001). [Review of the Motives, Values, Preferences Inventory]. In B. S. Plake & J. C. Impara (Eds.), *The fourteenth mental measurements yearbook.* Lincoln, NE: Buros Institute of Mental Measurements.

Roe, A. (1956). *The psychology of occupations.* New York: Wiley.

Roe, A. (1957). Early determinants of vocational choice. *Journal of Counseling Psychology, 4,* 212-217.

Roe, A., & Siegelman, M. (1964). *Origin of interests.* (APGA Inquiry Studies No. 1). Washington, DC: American Personnel and Guidance Association.

Rokeach, M. (1973). *The nature of human values.* New York: Free Press.

Rosen, S. D., Weiss, D. J., Hendel, D. D., Dawis, R. V., & Lofquist, L. H. (1972). *Occupational Reinforcer Patterns* (Vol. 2). (Minnesota Studies in Vocational Rehabilitation Monograph No. 29). Minneapolis, MN: Industrial Relations Center, University of Minnesota.

Rounds, J. B. (1995). Vocational interests: Evaluating structural hypotheses. In R. V. Dawis & D. Lubinski (Eds.), *Assessing individual differences in human behavior: New concepts, methods, and findings* (pp. 177-232.) Minneapolis, MN: University of Minnesota Press.

Rounds, J. B., Davison, M. L., & Dawis, R. V. (1979). The fit between Strong-Campbell Interest Inventory General Occupational Themes and Holland's hexagonal model. *Journal of Vocational Behavior, 15,* 303-315.

Rounds, J. B., & Zevon, M. A. (1983). Multidimensional scaling research in vocational psychology. *Applied Psychological Measurement, 7,* 491-510.

Schletzer, V. A. (1966). SVIB as a predictor of job satisfaction. *Journal of Applied Psychology, 50,* 5-8.

Schneider, B. (1987). The people make the place. *Personnel Psychology, 40,* 437-453.

Schultz, I. T., & Barnabas, B. (1945). Testing for leadership in industry. *Transactions of the Kansas Academy of Science, 4,* 160-164.

Spranger, E. (1928). *Types of men: The psychology and ethics of personality.* Halle: Max Niemeyer Verlag.

Strong, E. K., Jr. (1935). Predictive value of the Vocational Interest Test. *Journal of Educational Psychology, 26,* 332.

Strong. E. K., Jr. (1943). *Vocational interests of men and women.* Stanford, CA: Stanford University Press.

Strong, E. K., Jr. (1955). *Vocational interests 18 years after college.* Minneapolis, MN: University of Minnesota Press.

Strong, E. K., Jr. (1960). An 18-year longitudinal report on interests. In W. L. Layton (Ed.), *The Strong Vocational Interest Blank: Research and uses.* Minneapolis, MN: University of Minnesota Press.

Super, D. E. (1973). The Work Values Inventory. In D. G. Zytowski (Ed.), *Contemporary approaches to interest measurement.* Minneapolis, MN: University of Minnesota Press.

Super, D. E., & Crites, J. O. (1962). *Appraising vocational fitness.* New York: HarperCollins.

Tracey, T. J., & Rounds, J. (1992). *Evaluating Holland's and Gati's vocational interest models: A structural meta-analysis.* Paper presented at the 100th annual meeting of the American Psychological Association, Washington, DC.

Trimble, J. T. (1965). *Ten-year longitudinal follow-up study of inventoried interests of selected high school students.* Unpublished doctoral dissertation, University of Missouri.

U.S. Census Bureau, American FactFinder Population Estimates Program. (2006). *General demographic characteristics: July 2006.* Washington, DC: U.S. Census Bureau.

U.S. Department of Labor. (1991). *Dictionary of occupational titles.* Washington, DC: U.S. Government Printing Office.

Watson, G., & Glaser, E. M. (1980). *Watson-Glaser Critical Thinking Appraisal manual.* San Antonio, TX: Psychological Corporation.

Weaver, C. N. (1980). Job satisfaction in the United States in the 1970s. *Journal of Applied Psychology, 65,* 364-367.

Wiggins, J. D., & Weslander, D. L. (1979). Personality characteristics of counselors rated as effective or ineffective. *Journal of Vocational Behavior, 15,* 175-185.

Worthington, E. L., Jr., & Dolliver, R. H. (1977). Validity studies of the Strong Vocational Interest Inventories. *Journal of Counseling Psychology, 24,* 208-216.

Zedeck, S. (2001). [Review of the Motives, Values, Preferences Inventory]. In B. S. Plake & J. C. Impara (Eds.), *The fourteenth mental measurements yearbook*. Lincoln, NE: Buros Institute of Mental Measurements.

Zytowski, D. G. (1976). Predictive validity of the Kuder Occupational Interest Survey: A 12- to 19-year follow-up. *Journal of Counseling Psychology, 23,* 221-233.

Zytowski, D. G., & Kuder, F. (1986). Advances in the Kuder Occupational Interest Survey. In W. B. Walsh & S. H. Osipow (Eds.), *Advances in vocational psychology: Volume 1. The assessment of interest* (pp. 31-54). Hillsdale, NJ: Erlbaum.